Consistency in cognitiv
social behaviour

AF777264

Introductions to Modern Psychology

General Editor: Max Coltheart,
Birkbeck College, University of London

The Construction of Personality: An Introduction, Sarah Hampson

Clinical Psychopathology: An Introduction, E.M. Coles

Consistency in cognitive social behaviour

An introduction to social psychology

C.J.Mower White

Routledge & Kegan Paul
London, Boston, Melbourne and Henley

First published in 1982
by Routledge & Kegan Paul Ltd
39 Store Street, London WC1E 7DD,
9 Park Street, Boston Mass. 02108, USA,
296 Beaconsfield Parade, Middle Park,
Melbourne, 3206, Australia and
Broadway House, Newtown Road
Henley-on-Thames, Oxon RG9 1EN
Set in IBM Baskerville by
Thames Typesetting, Abingdon
and printed in Great Britain by
T.J. Press (Padstow) Ltd
Padstow, Cornwall
© C.J. Mower White 1982
No part of this book may be reproduced in
any form without permission from the
publisher, except for the quotation of brief
passages in criticism

Library of Congress Cataloging in Publication Data

Mower–White, C.J.

Consistency in cognitive social behaviour.
(Introductions to modern psychology)
Bibliography: p.
Includes index.
1. Social psychology. 2. Cognition – Social
aspects. I. Title. II. Series.
HM251.M67 302 82-445

ISBN 0-7100-9028-5 AACR2
ISBN 0-7100-9029-3 (pbk)

Contents

Acknowledgments

I am very grateful to thc following for their help which enabled this book to be written: Sarah Hampson and Max Coltheart for reading earlier drafts of the manuscript; Angus McLachlan and particularly Dick Eiser for providing much instruction and information without which this book would have taken a different form; and finally Helen, for being sleepy.

1 Cognitive social psychology: what is it, and how should it be done?

I Social psychology and cognitive social psychology

Perhaps one of the most important and obvious things about people is that they live and interact with each other. The social character of human behaviour is undeniable, and it is only the absence of social characteristics of behaviour which is remarkable; for example, living as a hermit or recluse is more than unusual, and may cause the more conventional to wonder about the sanity of this bizarre way of life. If social behaviour is such a common occurrence, then one might imagine that the study of it (which constitutes social psychology) is a very obvious subject, in that we may know a great deal about it simply by observing our own and each others' behaviour. To a certain extent this is true; it would be impossible to interact with others effectively without operating, at least some of the time, as a lay social psychologist. If this is so, it raises two points which need discussion before the main subject matter of this book is introduced. First, if we are all reasonably successful lay social psychologists, what is the need for, or function of, the professionals? Second, and more interestingly, how is it that as laymen we are *able* to be social psychologists? This second question may be expressed differently: what is the nature of those of our cognitive processes which allow us to interact with each other?

The first point could be answered in a number of ways. Professional social psychologists, some would argue, are concerned with a systematic analysis of people's behaviour as it is influenced by others, and traditionally the method used for such analysis has been experimental. Laymen would scarcely find experimental or even systematic methods feasible. A rather different answer might be that social psychology is an academic subject in its own right, and has no need to justify itself in terms of its application or function. Opposing this view is a now growing trend to consider that social psychology should be directly concerned with problems of human welfare (e.g. Billig, 1977; Ring, 1967). The opinion that social psychology should be applied originated with Lewin (1948), who is also responsible for the experimental and academic nature of the subject. However, later social psychologists (e.g. McGuire, 1965) believed that these different aspects of the subject could not be combined successfully. This problem, and in particular severe criticisms of the experimental method (e.g. Armistead, 1974; Gergen, 1973; Harré and Secord, 1972; Moscovici, 1972; Ring, 1967), has led to a debate within social psychology about the methodology which should be used. Some of the points of this debate, and the alternatives to the experimental method, will be considered later in this chapter.

The second question to be considered really forms the main topic of this book. When one asks how it is that laymen are able to be social psychologists, one is interested in the cognitive processes which take place when a person interacts with, or thinks about, another person, and so makes a prediction about the other's behaviour. The subject matter, then, of *cognitive* social psychology is what individuals *think* about social issues and people (including themselves), rather than their overt social *behaviour.* The topics which are generally included in a study of cognitive social psychology are the following: *attitudes* (see Chapter 2); *attribution,* or how we ascribe certain characteristics to other people or ourselves (see Chapter 3); and *attraction,* that is, how and why we like particular people, but not others (see Chapter 4). Chapter 5 will consider how these processes can be extended and affected by group membership: that is, how decisions about attitudes, attribution and attraction, are influenced by a person being part of a group of people who may be similar to himself.

2 Consistency in cognitive social psychology

When one considers these topics, there appears to be a simple general principle which has been used by social psychologists to explain them all. This is the notion of consistency. It seems that laymen and professional social psychologists alike expect that the different attitudes a person holds will be consistent with each other, that his attitudes will in turn be consistent with his behaviour, that he may be described by compatible or non-contradictory personality characteristics, and that he will be attracted to others who hold values consistent with his own. Consistency is probably an over-used word in social psychology, and may be taken to mean 'compatible', 'similar', 'non-contradictory', 'conforming', 'in agreement', or 'congruous'. These uses will be followed here.

There are several points to be made about the notion of consistency. As already mentioned it has been applied to a number of areas in social psychology and in personality theory. For instance, it sometimes appears that there are a number of personality traits which are similar in meaning and which are often found clustered together. For example, it might be that individuals who are shy are also timid and cautious, whereas those who are extroverted may be neighbourly and chatty. An important point about the idea of consistent clusters of traits (see Hampson, 1982), and about the notion of consistency generally, is that, although the concept of consistency may be based on fact, it is a notion which is exaggerated by the layman in his attempts to interpret and predict other people's behaviour; that is to say, it may be true that a person's attitudes are sometimes consistent with his behaviour, but it is likely that as laymen or as psychologists we expect this consistency more often than it is actually present.

A further question, then, must be concerned with the function of consistency, particularly if our expectations of it seldom mirror what is present. It seems that if we are using cognitive processes in order to make our social interactions more efficient, an important use of such cognition will be to predict other people's behaviour. After all, one cannot be particularly efficient at any activity unless one has some idea about how it is to be done. It is the same when, for example, chatting to a friend; by predicting his possible answers to one's remarks, one can guide the conversation so that it is pleasant and conflict-free. But what is the foundation for this prediction? This prediction is based on the notion of consistency. Knowing that people have tended to be consistent in their attitudes, values and behaviour in the past, we exaggerate this tendency, and expect them to be so in the future. This expectation allows us to predict not just that people will be consistent, but that they may have particular values and attitudes. Suppose, for example, that your new neighbour regularly takes his dog for a walk each morning. You might be justified in assuming that he is a dog-lover since this attitude would be consistent with his behaviour. You might further assume that it would not induce good neighbourly relations if you were to make loud remarks through the adjoining hedge, to the effect that rabies will soon be endemic among the dog population of this country. This further assumption also involves the notion of consistency and can be readily explained by the Balance theory of Heider (1958), discussed in Chapter 2. These assumptions are likely to guide your behaviour towards the neighbour, and, in turn, to influence the neighbour's behaviour towards you. For example, if he perceives that you are antagonistic to his dog, then he may be more covert, or more flaunting, in his morning walk, depending on whether he wishes to be friendly or hostile. It may be, of course, that your initial assumption was incorrect: perhaps he is *not* a dog-lover. Perhaps he keeps a dog because his wife fears burglars or to chase away the rats. This would then be an example of inconsistency between attitudes and behaviour, which in fact is fairly common (see Chapter 2). Nevertheless, your assumptions were based upon consistency, and it is this which allows maximum guidance of one's own and prediction of others' behaviour.

The important function of this expectation of consistency is, then, prediction and guidance of behaviour. A second function is related to the first. Since we expect others to be consistent, we value them when they are so. This becomes evident when listening to a person (perhaps oneself) dismiss another's opinion as 'inconsistent', with the implication that it is therefore not worth considering. Only consistent arguments have value, and similarly only people who are consistent in their attitudes, attributes and behaviour are regarded favourably.

This relationship of consistency and value may similarly be applied to oneself. Eiser (1971a) proposed that the tendency towards forming consistent expectations is an attempt 'to construct reality in such a way that one's self esteem is preserved or enhanced' (p.446). This proposal is supported by evidence (Eiser and Mower White 1974a; 1975) that people give more consistent descriptions of statements of opinion about an attitudinal issue when they are able to describe their own attitudes in more positively evaluative terms, so enhancing their own self esteem (see Chapter 2). Thus it seems that by using consistency to guide our own, and to predict other people's, future behaviour we may also be inducing and supporting our own self esteem.

3 Traditional social psychology and its problems

Traditionally, social psychology has been an experimental discipline, in which the investigator has been interested in the effect of different variables on social behaviour. For example he might be interested in how a person's opinions may be changed if he listens to people delivering persuasive speeches about a social issue. If such opinion change occurs, the investigator could manipulate certain variables and assess the degree of opinion change. Thus he could investigate the effect of the strength with which an opinion is initially held upon the degree to which it might be changed by the experimental treatment; or he could manipulate levels of involvement in the issue and see how this affected degree of opinion change. Alternatively, he could vary the nature of persuasive speech. Hovland and Weiss (1952) manipulated the credibility of the person delivering the speech, and demonstrated that a highly credible person is more influential in changing opinions than one of low credibility.

While one could not seriously challenge the commonsense nature of such a result, it is clear that experiments of this type pay little regard to the *subject* of the experiment – that is, to the person whose behaviour is being observed. A series of challenges to this utterly experimental approach began with the work on experimental artifacts and demand characteristics of experiments (e.g. Orne, 1962; Rosenthal and Rosnow, 1969); this work suggested that there may be a variety of confounding factors influencing social behaviour in the restrictive conditions of the laboratory. These factors primarily emerge from the subject himself, in the sense that they may be a product of the interpretation he gives to the experimental situation he is in. For example, subject's behaviour may be influenced by experimenter's sex (e.g. Glixman, 1967) and small differences in experimental instructions (e.g. Willems and Clark, 1969).

These criticisms are important because they have caused social psychologists to think more deeply about their methods of investigation and the direction of their discipline. It is therefore necessary to look at the problems traditional social psychology has faced; at some of the suggestions for revising the experimental method; and at the views of those who have proposed non-experimental methods of investigation.

A common criticism of experimental social psychology (e.g. Armistead, 1974; Jahoda, 1972; Moscovici, 1972; Ring, 1967) is that it has deserted its early direction, and no longer pays attention to the investigation of social *problems*. Jahoda (1972), in advancing this kind of criticism, has claimed that the discipline has confined itself to elegant trivialities. Ring (1967) has criticized the frivolity and 'fun and games' values implicit in many experiments, arguing that not only did this approach ignore problems of broad human significance, but that it led to students becoming bored and disenchanted with the subject, and, since a topic was dropped when no longer amusing, a number of areas of social psychology were only partly researched before being abandoned.

Moscovici (1972) argued that traditional experimental social psychology is often far from social in the sense that it is not concerned as it should be with man *in* society, and nor does it study social behaviour as an interaction between man and society. Instead, it appears to be interested in how a person reacts to social, as opposed to non-social stimuli; or even how people may be differentiated by their personality characteristics. Such studies, he claims, are not social:

> The proper domain of our discipline is the study of cultural processes which are responsible for the organization of knowledge in a society, for the establishment of inter-individual relationships ... for the formation of social movements ... for the codification of inter-individual and inter-group conduct which creates a common social reality with its norms and values, the origin of which is to be sought again in the social context. (pp. 55-6)

Moscovici's plea is for social psychology to be concerned with the study of communication, since the most important feature of human social behaviour is our use of symbols in social communication. This in turn produces ideologies, which are intricately bound up with communication. It is these two aspects of behaviour – ideology and communication – which should, according to Moscovici, form the basis of social psychology. This is so, since ideologies, produced by communication, initiate new conditions of social life, which in turn produce new types of social behaviour.

Moscovici's further concern with how social psychology may be a more adequate discipline relates to the role of theories in the discipline. He asserts that what is needed are theories which will allow sets of propositions to be systematized, and which offer new ideas whose worth can subsequently be assessed. Any thought provoking theory, he suggests, would be preferable to none at all, and the proposal of any such theory would be a more acceptable contribution to the discipline than the collection of trivial, piecemeal data from academically respectable experiments.

Finally, he claims that social psychologists must be prepared to abandon their traditionally scientific method and be ready to achieve their aims using a variety of approaches, which may be, among others, mathematical, observational or reflective. At present, the handicap of social psychology, according to Moscovici, is its inability to free itself from respectable science, so making it able to tackle only minor problems.

Other doubts concerning experiments in social psychology have been voiced by Tajfel (1972); these involve the interpretation which the subject makes of the experimental context. The problem, in essence, is that however many extraneous variables, social or non-social, an experimenter eliminates from the experiment, he cannot eliminate subjects' expectations about what is appropriate behaviour in this particular context. What is of crucial importance here, Tajfel argues, is the *social context*, embodied in those social expectations which are shared by most or all subjects entering an experiment. Since the social context is concerned with appropriate behaviour, and since 'to behave appropriately is a powerful social motive' (p.101), Tajfel considers that social psychologists must be aware that the social context is of prime importance in determining the data of any experiment. It is therefore necessary to realize that social psychological hypotheses cannot be stated in universal terms, because the social context, though it must by definition be shared, is unlikely to be universal. Social psychology should therefore be aiming to establish the values and norms relating to any particular behaviour, and an experimenter must consider who shares them, and in what situations they are relevant.

4 Variations on the experimental method in social psychology

These criticisms of, and problems with, traditional experimental social psychology have in recent years led to a number of variations on the experimental method, and in addition the rejection of experimentation in favour of other means of investigation. This section will consider the variations upon the experimental method which have been proposed; the next section will consider non-experimental methods of investigation.

One approach to the avoidance of the pitfalls of the traditional experiment was proposed by Rosenberg (1969). Although a behavourist, he acknowledged nevertheless that subjects might engage in purposeful activity in an attempt to interpret any situation including experimental situations. He believed that this could be eliminated by improved experimental techniques and by investigating influence processes within the experiment. Thus by experiments about experiments spurious casual factors inherent in the design could be removed.

Unfortunately this approach, though successful in eliminating the more obvious biases of the laboratory, could not remove the possibility that the sheer awareness of being in an experiment might alter subjects' behaviour. Furthermore, this approach did not deal with the problem posed by Tajfel (1972), that subjects' interpretation of what is appropriate behaviour is a vital influence on the data yielded by any social-psychological experiment.

A rather different view which has been proposed is that the influence of the laboratory situation is too pervasive for the results to be generalized to other situations, and that in an experiment subjects' interpretations might be crucial. One of the proponents of this approach was Campbell (1969), who suggested that problems arising from a subject's awareness that he was participating in an experiment might be avoided by using naturalistic experiments. One such experiment, in which subjects were unaware they were being observed by experimenters, was that of Darley and Latané (1968). This study was concerned with bystander intervention, and used a contrived emergency in which subjects overheard a fellow subject simulating an epileptic fit. The majority of subjects who believed that they were alone in hearing the emergency reported it, while those who thought that they were one of a number who were able to hear it rarely did so. Darley and Latané suggested that diffusion of responsibility might explain these results. An isolated individual can avoid feeling guilty by trying to help, but one subject among several hearing the emergency may be more concerned about making a fool of himself in front of others and is likely to be guided by the others' behaviour when deciding whether to help.

While this experiment has become a classic in the study of bystander intervention and altruism, as a model for other areas in social psychology it has three major drawbacks. First, natural settings severely restrict the range of behaviour which can be observed without the subject's knowledge that he is in an experiment. For example, one can scarcely imagine investigating much of cognitive social behaviour using this method since it is often unavailable to an observer unless he asks specifically prepared questions. Second, there are ethical considerations which investigators observing certain, if not all, aspects of behaviour without the subjects' knowledge must face.[1] Third, it is not necessarily the case that results from natural experiments can be generalized to all types of natural settings; it is merely that subjects' awareness of being in an experiment can be avoided.

The final approach to the avoidance of the disadvantages of traditional experimentation is typified by the work of Tajfel (1972). As already discussed, Tajfel considered that the subject must be treated as an interpretive agent, and that an experimenter must be aware that his procedures may affect social behaviour within the experiment. In this approach, then, the social significance of the experimental setting is particularly important. Further, Tajfel maintains that social psychological theories which are open to experimental test contain the most hopeful promise for the future. In addition to stressing a reliance on experimental method, he proposes that one can overcome its difficulties by developing theories which encompass the context in which social behaviour occurs.

5 Non-experimental methods of investigation

When one considers the problems and criticisms of traditional experimental social psychology which have just been discussed, it is scarcely surprising that some solutions advocate complete rejection of the experimental method and of the idea of a science of social behaviour based on observable facts. The most complete statement of this rejectionist position was made by Harré and Secord (1972). The alternative they propose is called 'ethogeny'. Other rejectionist views have been advanced by Garfinkel (1967) and by Zimmerman and Pollner (1971), both of whom advocate an 'ethnomethodological' approach which has, as its base, methods which have been developed for studying problems within sociology. A further view, that of the symbolic interactionists (e.g. Blumer, 1969), claims to develop a sociological social psychology, and therefore has similarities with the other two approaches. These three non-experimental methods of investigation will now be examined briefly; particular attention will be paid to their similarities, and to the problems they have faced in finding workable paradigms for social psychology.

In describing these rejectionist approaches it is more difficult to be specific about the aims and methods they advocate, than about their criticisms of traditional experimentation in social psychology. The most complete statement of all the rejectionist approaches, was made by Harré and Secord (1972), and opposes a positivistic science of social behaviour. In place of observable facts, the data for ethogeny consists of 'accounts', or self-reports, of subjects' behaviour. Harré and Secord claim that a subject's own commentary on his behaviour is an authentic form of data, which may nevertheless be revised by the investigator through negotiation with the subject. The meaning of social behaviour is important for ethogeny (as it is for other rejectionist approaches); social behaviour should not, therefore, be analysed or reduced to non-meaningful elements, but should be examined at the level at which the subject understands and reports his behaviour and social interactions. It appears that ethogeny, as other rejectionist positions, is anxious to respect its subjects and *not* to treat them as mere mechanisms whose behaviour can be explained by 'a combination of the effects of external stimuli and prevailing organismic states' (Harré and Secord, 1972, p.30).

A similar emphasis is proposed by ethnomethodology: Garfinkel (1967) refers to the 'cultural dope' (p.68) described by traditional sociologists who expect people to behave in accordance with established patterns and therefore to reproduce stable features of society. Instead, the aim of ethnomethodology is to understand the meaning that people give to events themselves and the way that meanings are communicated. It is the intention of activities, rather than the results of those activities which should be of interest. According to Garfinkel (1967) and Schutz and Luckmann (1974) ethnomethodologists should follow the example of real people by making the assumption that other people are as they appear to be, and that others are essentially the same as themselves. Reality is therefore shared in the sense that consciousness is similar for other people. It follows from this that an investigator should abandon the attempt at objectivity and rationality, and should be trusting rather than sceptical of his subjects.

The symbolic interactionists have a similar emphasis on social reality and the meaning of social behaviour. Meltzer, Petras and Reynolds (1975) stress the importance of the meaning of social behaviour in outlining the tenets of symbolic interactionism: that people act towards things according to those things' perceived meanings; that meanings are produced by social interaction; and that meanings can be modified through interpretive processes. In a similar way to ethogenists and ethnomethodologists, the symbolic interactionists stress the use of symbols and, above all, language for social behaviour. Human interaction is mediated by language, and by ascertaining the meaning of another person's behaviour. Again, similar to the other two approaches, symbolic interactionists rely on their subjects' accounts or self reports for their data, and emphasize that an investigator should aim for a sympathetic understanding of his subjects.

The three rejectionist approaches can be broadly divided into two groups: ethogeny and symbolic interactionism are similar in their methodology and aims, while ethnomethodology has a somewhat different philosophical stance. The former two approaches claim that the traditional social psychologist is too divorced from the everyday world and manipulates passive subjects in a way which requires the psychologist to be deceitful. Ethogenists and symbolic interactionists obtain data from the reports of actors (or subjects), although ethogenists suggest that these accounts need not be accepted at face value. (How one is allowed to doctor them is not clear.) An investigator must respect the views of his subjects with whom he must have a sympathetic rapport. In the same vein, symbolic interactionists propose that it is possible to be both observer and observed, a proposal which would find little support in traditional social psychology. The aim of the ethogenists and symbolic interactionists is to discover the rules which underlie social behaviour with the implication that these rules (or norms) can be expressed. However, this in itself is insufficient for an ethogenic analysis: what is required is a description of the actor's wants, expectations and choice of rule.

Harré and Secord propose that, for an ethogenic analysis, the investigator should cease the attempt to control and predict, but should instead aim to *understand* behaviour and the meaning of social interaction. They criticize traditional social psychology on the now familiar grounds that the experimental method does not take account of the situation the subject is in, and that it is unable to develop concepts which allow the subject to be treated as an active causal agent.

Ethnomethodology finds an opposite fault with the traditional social psychologist, namely, that he *fails* to divorce himself from the everyday world. This approach demands that an investigator steps outside the normal social world and cuts himself off from his usual social ties. Garfinkel (1967), for example, asked students to act as lodgers in their own homes, so removing normal family ties and obligations and observing behaviour in a dissociated manner. A further criticism levelled by ethnomethodology is that traditional social psychology assumes the reality of a phenomenon, whereas this rejectionist position suggests that reality is not available to knowledge until perceptions have been organized and interpreted by an observer. While this phenomenological approach is rarely emphasized in social psychology, it is not new. The theory of Personal Constructs proposed by Kelly (1955) describes man as trying to make sense of the world by interpreting his perceptions according to his constructs, and is thus similarly a phenomenological theory.

The aims of ethnomethodology are concerned with the rational properties of everyday action and with discovering how people go about seeing, describing and explaining order in the world. It is claimed that ordinary people are 'lay sociologists', attempting to categorize and make sense of others' behaviour. This latter description again bears a remarkable similarity to the views of Kelly (1955), in which man is conceived of as trying to make sense of the world. Kelly's philosophical principle of Constructive Alternativism explains how constructs used for interpreting the world can be different for different people, and how such constructs can be revised in the face of new information or perceptions which do not fit with existing constructs. Kelly claims that 'Man is a Scientist' (p.4) since the aim of living is to predict and control events. This is done by making representations or constructions of reality. It appears that this philosophical stance is similar in essence to the claims of the ethnomethodologists. Further, one could assert that cognitive social psychologists are also in the business of understanding how people perceive, describe and explain order in the world, particularly that part of it which is concerned with people including themselves. The novelty of ethnomethodology then appears to be merely its methodological claims of detachment from the world, which is surely remarkably difficult to achieve, and of collecting data in the form of actors' reports, which it shares with ethogeny and symbolic interactionism.

In assessing these new methodologies, one criterion that could be used is the amount of new information that they have provided. None of the three has so far produced much concrete research that is relevant to social psychology (Billig, 1977). However, if, with Moscovici (1972), one believes that social psychologists might advantageously stop producing data in an effort to find a theory which will provide them with new ideas, this might not be too much of a problem. The new methodologies have, however, met with considerable difficulty in finding a workable research paradigm. Although social psychology might well benefit from a coherent philosophical stance, those methodologies which fail to provide a research paradigm are unlikely to be adopted very readily.

Further problems can be identified if one looks at the different methods of investigation individually. Gordon (1976) maintains that ethnomethodology suffers from being subjective, and that its findings cannot be confirmed, due to the nature of the approach and its methodology. Hindess (1973) argues that the phenomenological position of ethnomethodology, which asserts that reality is not available to knowledge other than after organization of perceptions and interpretation by an observer, leads to the denial of the possibility of rational knowledge. This is so since reality is only available to scientific inquiry in the form of observers' reports which are themselves subject to interpretation. This phenomenological position is again similar to that of Kelly (1955), but the latter's strength is that not only is his theory soundly based in philosophical principles, but that he provides a method (the repertory grid) by which a person's construct system can be investigated. Ethnomethodology lacks this sophistication.

More specific criticisms have been levelled at ethogeny. For example, data collected by asking actors to report on their actions implies that they can be accurate and objective. Shotter (1978) questions whether actors are always aware of the reasons for their action. A study in the tradition of experimental social psychology by Nisbett and Wilson (1977) suggested that subjects were often incapable of distinguishing the cognitive processes in which they had engaged, but instead explained their behaviour using rationalizations which they could have drawn from common sense, rather than from observation of their behaviour.

A similar claim is made by Farr (1977) in his comments on Herzlich's (1973) study of health and illness. Farr suggests that Herzlich's methodology is an example of the ethogenic approach since individuals gave open-ended accounts of their images of health and illness. The extensive interviews from which these accounts were obtained were guided in terms of themes to be explored, and the accounts, which were taken at face value, demonstrated that the self (constitution, heredity, temperament) is seen as the source of health, whereas the environment (in general, city life) is believed to be the source of illness. Farr argues that this method of collecting data could be expected to result in just such a conclusion if one pays attention to the work of Heider (1958) on the attribution of causality (see Chapter 3), in which he claims that favourable results are attributed to the self, whereas unfavourable results are attributed to external forces. Thus the problems for the ethogenic method are whether actors' accounts can include objective reasons for behaviour, and whether the resulting data are unduly influenced by the methodology, providing little more than commonsense rationalizations.

A more general criticism of the methodologies of the rejectionist views has been voiced by Billig (1977). He argues that the methods used give maximum emphasis to individuals' reasons for social behaviour, and that these may not be the best explanatory mechanisms. Using the example of fascism as a political movement, he shows that it is difficult to understand in terms with which individuals would describe their participation in that political activity. This type of methodology merely diverts attention from more powerful factors which are responsible for social behaviour at the wider collective level.

In summary, it must be concluded that the rejectionist methodologies have not so far been successful in social psychology, and seem unlikely to be so. This view is based on the arguments that they have not provided a competent workable paradigm, and that they replace more explanatory techniques, which have already demonstrated their worth at a collective level, merely substituting individual descriptions of behaviour.

6 Conclusion

In concluding, it is necessary to discuss which approach to the discipline is the most appropriate for cognitive social psychology. The problems which have faced social psychology in general are also applicable to that aspect of it which is concerned with cognition. If one is interested in how people think about social situations, social issues, and other people, one can scarcely deny that a person is capable of interpreting the social situation or the experiment he is in. The cognitive social psychologist must therefore allow for his subjects being interpretive and active causal agents.

However, some of the variations on the experimental method are simply not available to the cognitive social psychologist. A strict behaviourist methodology would presumably be unacceptable, although Bem (1965; 1967) has usefully adapted it in the study of attitudes and attribution (see Chapters 2 and 3). Similarly it is difficult to imagine a naturalistic experiment with the investigator observing a passive subject 'having an attitude'. Since the subject's overt behaviour may not be consistent with his attitude (see Chapter 2), it is generally recognized that the only way of knowing about a person's attitudes is to ask him about them, and it would be difficult to do this without his knowledge. The problems encountered by the new or rejectionist methods do not inspire a great deal of confidence in these approaches, and thus cognitive social psychology is forced to rely on the traditional experimental methods with the additions advocated by Tajfel (1972): the subject should be treated as an interpretive agent and the psychologist be aware that experimental procedures can affect the subject's behaviour.

Thus the most acceptable model of investigation for cognitive social psychology is one which uses an experimental method and allows an active model of man who interprets the social situation which he is in and acts accordingly. One must therefore develop theories which include and explain the context in which social behaviour occurs. Furthermore, it is necessary to be aware that experimental procedures may radically affect social behaviour, and that an experiment is a social situation of a rather special kind.

It is not necessarily the case, however, that all the experiments discussed in the following chapters have incorporated this approach into their methodology, and it is for the reader to judge whether investigators would have been more successful had they done so.

Finally, it is necessary to emphasize that the view of cognitive social psychology taken in this book is that consistency is the best explanatory mechanism which psychologists have yet provided to account for most aspects of cognitive social behaviour. In an attempt to demonstrate this, theories which utilize consistency principles, as well as those which do not, will be discussed in the following chapters. Theories of attitudes, attribution and attraction will be considered in the next three chapters, while Chapter 5 discusses how such processes are influenced by group membership. Finally, Chapter

6 examines what may happen if consistency is no longer an important determinant of cognitive social behaviour: humour, or the breakdown of social relationships.

Note

1 It may be considered that there are two independent ethical issues at stake in this situation. The first is the question of observing subjects when they are unaware that an experimenter is doing so. The second is the more specific issue of exposing people to, albeit simulated, epileptic fits, and allowing them to learn about their own reactions.

2 Consistency in attitudes

I Introduction

Much of social psychology has been devoted to the study of attitudes. Indeed, early writers such as Thomas and Znaniecki (1918) considered social psychology to be the scientific study of attitudes. While few social psychologists today would wish to exclude the many other aspects of their discipline, which has mushroomed alarmingly since that original limiting definition, nevertheless many are, and have been, involved in the study of attitudes.

There have been many definitions of attitude: for example Allport (1935) proposed that 'an attitude is a mental and neural state of readiness, organized through experience, exerting a directive or dynamic influence upon the individual's response to all objects and situations with which it is related' (p.810). While this definition certainly provides a formal description of the concept, it, and others like it, provide little more information than ideas attached to the word 'attitude' as used in common parlance. It seems doubtful, therefore, whether a formal definition is helpful.

Much of the work concerned with attitudes has investigated how the different attitudes that a person holds may be interrelated, and how his attitudes correspond to his behaviour. Attitude theories, which offer explanations of the interrelationships of attitudes, very often use consistency as a general principle: a person's attitudes are thought to be consistent with one another (e.g. Abelson and Rosenberg, 1958; Festinger, 1957; Heider, 1946, 1958; Newcomb, 1953, 1968;

Osgood and Tannenbaum, 1955). For example, such theories might predict that a child who enjoys going to school (i.e. has a positive attitude towards school), also likes his teacher (i.e. has a positive attitude towards her). There have been a number of such 'consistency' theories; those which have produced the most research will be examined in the first part of this chapter. The second part of the chapter will consider consistency, or lack of consistency, between attitudes and behaviour.

2 Balance Theory

The earliest of the attitude consistency theories, balance theory, comes from Heider (1946, 1958). The theory is concerned not with events themselves, but with an individual's perceptions of events and his expectations concerning them. Thus the interest is in, for example, what I believe my neighbour's attitude to cutting his grass may be, rather than in his actual attitude. It is therefore a theory of *cognitive* consistency, not implying that relationships between attitudes are logically consistent, but that people think they are. Consequently the theory would predict that I believe that my neighbour enjoys cutting his grass since I know (at least he told me) that he prefers his garden to look tidy. There is, of course, no logical necessity that my neighbour's attitudes should be consistent, and one could think of many reasons why they might not be; nevertheless, the initial expectation is one of consistency, at least according to the theory. Heider believed that cognitions about relationships, not necessarily the relationships themselves, give an understanding of social behaviour. These aspects of the theory are similar to those used by Heider to explain attraction (see Chapter 4); however in addition to his concept of 'dyadic balance', which will be explained in Chapter 4, 'triadic balance' plays an important part in the theory, not so much due to emphasis by Heider, as to emphasis that attitude research has placed upon it.

Heider's triads are usually described as being composed either of three people (P,O and Q), or two people (P and O) and an attitudinal object X, plus the relationships between the three entities. A triad is balanced if all three relationships (PO, OX and PX) are positive (e.g. liking, or approving of): for example, if I like Mr H and we both approve of the actions of a particular political party, the triad here is a balanced one. A balanced triad, or situation, may also result if two of the three relationships are negative (e.g. disliking or disapproving) and one is positive. For example: I like Ann (PO positive) and Ann and I both disapprove of the increasing population of dogs (X) (OX negative and PX negative). Alternatively, Ian dislikes Harry (PO negative) and while Harry likes John (OQ positive), Ian does not (PQ negative). Since Heider does not specify the position of the positive or negative relationships in the triad for balance to occur, there are four possible balanced triads, as shown in Figure 2.1.

Balanced		Unbalanced	
1	P + O + + X	5	P − O − − X
2	P + O − − X	6	P − O + + X
3	P − O − + X	7	P + O + − X
4	P − O + − X	8	P + O − + X

\+ represents a positive relationship (e.g. liking, approving)
− represents a negative relationship (e.g. dislike, disapproving)

FIGURE 2.1 Heider's (1958) balanced and unbalanced triads

Similarly, there are four possible unbalanced triads (also shown in Figure 2.1). Three of those result from situations in which two relationships are positive and one is negative. For example, suppose I like my neighbour (PO positive) and yet we cannot agree about the best height for our adjoining fence (OX positive and PX negative). A fourth form of unbalanced triad is that shown in Figure 2.1 (no. 5) in which all three relationships are negative. Heider actually considered this situation ambiguous, but the majority of later researchers have included it among the unbalanced triads.

Heider suggests that balanced triads are pleasant situations in which there is harmony, lack of tension and no pressure to change any of the relationships. In unbalanced triads there is a tendency to change one relationship so that balance results. Similarly, as balanced states are preferable to unbalanced, an incomplete triad is, theoretically, completed so as to be balanced. Thus in outlining his theory Heider provides specific ways in which it may be tested, and subsequent research has used his proposals. Data are often in the form of pleasantness ratings of balanced and unbalanced triads; alternatively subjects may be asked to predict a change in any of the relationships, or to predict a third relationship in an incomplete triad.

An experiment in which subjects were asked to rate the pleasantness of different balanced and unbalanced triads was reported by Mower White (1977a). Subjects were given a questionnaire which described eight situations, corresponding to the eight possible triads formed from positive and negative relations in each position in the triad, and asked to rate each for pleasantness. In one condition person P was described as 'you' (i.e. the subject), whereas in the other condition P was an arbitrary boy's name. In both conditions, O and Q were other arbitrary boys' names. Balance theory was supported in the former condition but not in the latter, suggesting that a subject must be identified with a member of the triad for the balance bias to be effective.

A number of studies have investigated balance theory by asking subjects to predict a change in any of the relationships (e.g. Rodrigues, 1967), or a third relationship in an incomplete triad (e.g. Rodrigues, 1968). The former tended to support the theory when OX was changed, and the latter when there was no strong pressure towards agreement. In other words, subjects did not necessarily predict a balanced situation: only when they chose to change the OX relationship (which does not involve the subject), and when experimental details did not specify a strong requirement for agreement (between P and O, about X) in the triad was Heider's theory supported.

Another group of studies (Zajonc and Burnstein, 1965; Zajonc and Sherman, 1967; Rubin and Zajonc, 1969; Cottrell, Ingraham and Monfort, 1971; Sherman and Wolosin, 1973), asked subjects to learn relationships in complete triads, using paired associates learning. Subjects were thus presented with, for example, two names (e.g. 'Bob' and 'Bill') representing P and O and then told the relationship between them (e.g. 'likes'). On subsequent presentations of these names subjects had to respond with the correct relationship. This methodology was based on the view proposed by Zajonc and Burnstein that balance is a 'social schema' (Kuethe, 1962), or a strong or good *Gestalt* (Jordan, 1953). Triads were thus thought to be more likely to be balanced, and therefore balanced triads learned more easily than unbalanced. This view presumably held that a more likely occurrence is learned more readily. These experiments in no way give the theory unequivocal support. In general they showed few balance effects (with the exception of the work of Zajonc and Burnstein which supported Balance theory when an involving issue (X) was used, but which could not be replicated by Rubin and Zajonc).

A general conclusion which may be drawn from these studies, and many others testing balance theory, is that it has only limited experimental support, which can be attributable to fairly definite conditions (Mower White, 1979). For example, the subject must identify himself with a member of the triad (Mower White, 1977a), and the triad should be presented as a unified structure (Sherman and Wolosin, 1973). This later condition was not fulfilled by the learning experiments mentioned above, and it is scarcely surprising that subjects would not expect balance in structures which are presented as a series of single relationships which have no obvious connections between them. A further condition appears to be that the triad should be in a relatively simple context (Mower White, 1977b), so that subjects are not given too much information from which to abstract the relevant relationships of the triad.

Apart from the lack of complete support for balance theory, there are other points which can be mentioned relating to it. At first glance it may appear that the theory is not elaborate enough to require diagrams of triads and symbols such as P, O and X. It really is one of the simplest theories in social psychology, and in essence merely states that we prefer to agree with our friends, and to disagree with those whom we dislike. Intuitively, people very often believe that this is right, which is an advantage for the theory, since it is one of *cognitive* consistency: if we did not believe that what it predicted was accurate then it would almost certainly be inaccurate. However, although it is a simple theory which sounds right, empirically it is too simple, since there are only particular conditions under which it is supported. Being too simple, it has been modified and over-shadowed by more elaborate theories; but balance theory nevertheless remains the earliest and most basic of the attitude theories, and the theory from which the remainder stem.

3 Newcomb's (1968) theory of interpersonal balance

Newcomb's (1968) theory can fairly accurately be described as a modification of Heider's balance theory, and was proposed to account for data which the original theory did not explain. Both theories are explanations of cognitive consistency, but Newcomb assumed that an important concern in interpersonal relationships is the suitability of the other person as a source of information about, or support for, an attitude towards an object. Thus in the POX triad, it is important for P that O is a suitable influence on P's attitude to X. This suitability may be violated when O is ignorant of X, when PX does not concern O, or, most importantly, when P does not like O. In this latter point the theory differs most explicitly from that of Heider, since Newcomb proposes that when P does not like O, O is not a suitable influence on PX, and P is therefore indifferent to the POX triad, causing a state of 'non-balance'. The remaining two states of balance roughly conform to Heider's conceptions, except that, of necessity, they are both characterized by positive PO relations, and termed 'positively balanced', and 'positively imbalanced'.

In terms of the triads illustrated in Figure 2.1, those with negative PO relationships, (i.e. triads 3, 4, 5 and 6) are termed 'non balanced' by Newcomb. Positively balanced triads (nos 1 and 2) have positive PO relationships and agreement between P and O concerning X (PX and OX are either both positive or both negative). Newcomb differs from Heider in that he does not use the term 'unbalanced'; his positively imbalanced triads (nos 7 and 8) are characterized by a positive PO relationship and disagreement between P and O (PX and OX differ, one being positive and the other negative).

A number of studies have been claimed as support for Newcomb's as opposed to Heider's theory: (e.g. Crano and Cooper, 1973; Fuller, 1974; Gerard and Fleischer, 1967; Jordan, 1953; Price, Harburg and Newcomb, 1966). However it is not certain that greater confidence should be placed in the more recent theory. An additional complication arises when one considers that Heider's balance is formed from an interaction between agreement and PO positivity; both or neither must be present for a triad to be balanced. Many studies (e.g. Gutman and Knox, 1972; Jordan, 1953; Rubin and Zajonc, 1969; Whitney, 1971; Zajonc and Burnstein, 1965) have indicated that triads containing PO positivity are preferable, less tension provoking, or more easily learned than those in which PO is negative, *irrespective* of the other relations in the triad. This so-called 'positivity bias' is not particularly surprising: it simply suggests that we prefer to be in situations in which we like somebody. In addition, an 'agreement bias' has been shown (e.g. Aderman, 1969: Insko, Songer and McGarvey, 1974; Rodrigues, 1968; Whitney, 1971) such that triads in which P and O agree about Q or X are more pleasant or more expected than when there is disagreement. Newcomb's claim that only positively balanced triads (i.e. triads 1 and 2, in Figure 2.1) are pleasant, while positively imbalanced triads (i.e. triads 7 and 8) are unpleasant could be empirically correct, but due to faulty reasoning. It seems likely that positively balanced triads are preferable because they are characterized by a positive PO relationship, agreement and Heiderian balance, all of which tend to make a triad pleasant. Similarly positively imbalanced triads are unpleasant probably because they are neither balanced, nor contain agreement. Non-balanced triads (nos 3, 4, 5 and 6 in Figure 2.1) are either balanced or contain agreement, but not both, and receive an intermediate rating, or, as Newcomb predicts, one of indifference.

The problem of this confounding of biases in Newcomb's theory, means that his threefold classification does not allow an adequate demonstration of the effect of various social situations in priming particular biases. Thus certain situations – e.g. a minority position in an important argument, as in the study by Rodrigues (1968) – have an effect of priming the agreement bias, so making agreement in the triad a more likely event. Such situations cannot be investigated using Newcomb's classification, whereas Heider's classification does allow them to be examined, even though it makes no allowance for varying social situations (Mower White, 1979).

Such a consideration again raises the question of whether Heider's theory is too simple. It can be easily demonstrated (e.g. Crockett, 1974; Mower White, 1977a, 1979; Rodrigues, 1968; Yang and Yang, 1973) that varying social conditions can vary the support for balance theory, and that attitudes may be consistent with expectations about social conditions and not necessarily balanced as Heider implied. Data of this sort do not support Heider because he failed to consider the social context of his triads. At the same time such data substantiate the movement which Heider began; that is, we expect attitudes to be consistent with each other *and* with the social situation which appears most relevant to them.

Heider's theory may also be seen as too simple in that it has, as the earliest consistency theory, been surpassed by a number of others, many of which have used its basic tenets with relatively minor qualifications (e.g. Newcomb, 1968). Others (e.g. Festinger, 1957) have taken the consistency framework and elaborated what amounts to a whole school of social psychology. With such simple beginnings to the attitude theories this situation is probably inevitable. However, as will be seen later in this chapter, attitude theories which do not utilize Heider's basic principle of consistency do not have much support.

4 Cognitive dissonance theory

Festinger's (1957) theory is probably better known than Heider's balance theory in that it has produced more research, and, more recently, has led to a number of developments (e.g. Bem, 1967; Nuttin, 1975), which cannot be claimed by Heider. It is also a more formally stated theory than that of Heider, but again, like balance theory, it deals with cognitive consistency, that is, with beliefs, values attitudes, ideas and opinions, and is therefore best known in the field of attitude research.

Festinger held cognitive dissonance to be 'a negative drive state occurring when an individual holds two cognitions which are psychologically inconsistent' (1957, p.13). If there are two cognitions X and Y, and if the opposite of cognition Y 'follows from' (Festinger's term) cognition X, then X and Y are psychologically inconsistent, and dissonance will be experienced. When a person experiences such dissonance, he will reduce it in one of two ways: either by changing one of the cognitions, or by adding another. Thus the knowledge that 'I smoke' (one cognition) and the belief that 'smoking causes lung cancer' (a second cognition) may result in dissonance, which can be reduced either by changing one of the cognitions (e.g. stopping smoking) or by adding a further one (e.g. 'smoking calms my nerves').

The original statement of dissonance theory received a great deal of criticism, primarily from Chapanis and Chapanis (1964). One of the problems they demonstrated is that it is sometimes not quite clear when dissonance will arise. Festinger claimed that, in his definition, 'follows from' means psychologically related, maybe through past experience, cultural values or some logical relationship, but very often it is still difficult to be precise about when dissonance will arise. Aronson's (1968) example (p.9) is useful here: if you are told that your favourite novelist beats his wife, does this arouse dissonance? The two cognitions (X is my favourite novelist, and X beats his wife) are not dissonant according to Festinger's proposals although one may presume that being a good novelist involves being compassionate and sympathetic and that these are inconsistent with wife beating. However, there is no *logical* inconsistency, nor inconsistency with past experience nor cultural values, in that there is no specific value according to which it is desirable that novelists do not beat their wives. Aronson suggests that it is preferable to say that dissonance is induced if one cognition violates an expectancy of the other.

The late 1950s and early 1960s produced a large volume of research into dissonance theory, and the initial impression given is that the theory has been more prolific than balance theory, and can deal with more complicated phenomena. In addition, supporters of the theory pride themselves upon its ability to make 'non obvious' predictions – that is, dissonance can be resolved by ways which are not obvious at first sight. The best known example of this type of prediction concerns the celebrated medium Mrs Keech (Festinger, Riecken and Schachter, 1956), who received a message from the planet Clarion that a flood would destroy her city on a particular date. Mrs Keech and her followers, in the belief that they would be rescued on that date and taken away by a flying saucer, sold all their possessions and spent their money, thinking they would soon no longer need worldly wealth. When the date came, and there was no flood, and no flying saucer, their dissonance was resolved not, as one might expect, by discrediting Mrs Keech (i.e. changing a cognition) which would be the obvious prediction, but by the non-obvious method of adding a new cognition (Mrs Keech and her followers came to the view that the city was saved through their belief and action). The problem for the theory may be that it cannot predict which method of reducing dissonance is the more likely.

Much of the early dissonance research concerned 'forced compliance'; subjects being put in situations and asked to behave in ways which were contrary to their attitudes. Festinger proposed that such a condition should arouse dissonance, which would be reduced by a change of attitude, so as to be consistent with the behaviour concerned. Perhaps the best known experiment of this type, and one which has been repeated a number of times in various forms (e.g. see Chapter 3), is that of Festinger and Carlsmith (1959). In the original version of this experiment, subjects were given the intentionally boring task of putting twelve spools into a tray, emptying it, and refilling it, for one hour. They were then asked to participate in some deception: to tell the next subject (a stooge) that the task was interesting. Here there were two conditions. In the first condition, subjects were paid one dollar for the deception; in the second condition subjects were paid twenty dollars. Festinger and Carlsmith predicted that this experimental manipulation should produce dissonance in subjects in the first condition, the relevant dissonant cognitions being 'I'm being paid a trifling sum for telling my fellow subject a lie': and 'it's wrong to tell lies'. The dissonance here would be reduced by attitude change: 'I'm not telling lies; – it's true that the task is interesting.' Less dissonance was predicted in the second condition because twenty dollars was apparently thought sufficient payment for telling a lie. The attitude change was assessed by asking all subjects to rate the task on how interesting they found it, and, as predicted, those in the first condition rated the task more interesting than those in the second condition, who presumably considered twenty dollars enough money for the deception to be worthwhile.

After several years of experimentation an important attack on dissonance theory was made. These critical views, advanced by Chapanis and Chapanis (1964), claimed, firstly, that the theory was conceptually weak, citing, for example, the problem already mentioned of the meaning of 'follows from' in Festinger's original definition of dissonance. They also claimed that the theory was trying to explain too much, and that a theory with too wide a domain in fact explains very little. Perhaps their most serious criticisms concerned the experiments purporting to demonstrate the theory. These were said to be badly designed with manipulations which were often complex and confounded. They had, according to Chapanis and Chapanis, insufficient controls and dubious statistics. In addition many subjects had been eliminated from the analysis, and particularly those that did not conform to the predictions made by experimenters.

It is hardly surprising that such an attack had a serious effect on Festinger's theory. For some years little new research was produced in this area. However, dissonance theory is a remarkable example in social psychology of a theory which has overcome its criticisms by developing into a more useful and far reaching approach. The Chapanis paper was answered by Aronson (1968), who, in addition to clarifying various conceptual aspects of the theory, suggested that it might be more useful if limited to predictions about the self concept or other particularly strong expectancies. Thus if the self is involved in dissonant cognitions then Aronson's reformulation of the theory proposes that dissonance is likely to be reduced.

A more recent challenge to dissonance theory has come from Nuttin (1975) in a series of experiments designed to replicate the Festinger and Carlsmith (1959) study. Nuttin initially set out to test the assumption of dissonance theory that in a forced compliance situation a small incentive (e.g. one dollar) produces more attitude change than a large incentive (e.g. twenty dollars), the smaller being just sufficient to elicit counter-attitudinal behaviour, but not large enough to provide justification for compliance. Nuttin repeated a modified form of the Festinger and Carlsmith study, but introduced a control condition in which no incentive was paid, and an additional condition in which subjects were told that they could not be paid because funds were now used up, even though previous subjects had received money. The small incentive condition produced attitude change as Festinger would predict, while the control condition and large incentive condition showed no attitude change. However in the additional condition subjects showed even greater change than those given a small incentive causing Nuttin to argue that it is not giving a large incentive which reduced dissonance but that the unfair withholding of reward, or giving unfairly low reward produces dissonance.

A further experiment in Nuttin's series extended this conclusion. The (female) experimenter intentionally dressed in 'embarrassing clothes' (very short hot pants and low-necked T shirt) which were completely unacceptable at the time particularly in a work setting in a Catholic university. The embarrassed subjects were asked to write essays or creative pieces either in favour or against a reform of the examination system before their attitudes were assessed. Nuttin argued that the embarrassing conditions of dress lead to arousal, and that attitude responses (i.e. the essays or creative writing) produced under conditions of arousal generalize to later attitude testing situations, such that those asked to write in favour of reform were later more in favour than those asked to write against the reform. Nuttin likens his results to those of the experiment by Schachter and Singer (1962) in which emotional states were seen as a function of physiological arousal *and* of a particular cognition or label which the subject attaches to that arousal, and suggests that response contagion is preferable to dissonance as an explanation of attitude change. Thus the explanation in terms of response contagion proposes that the presence of an arousing stimulus (e.g. embarrassing experimenter, too little reward, or no reward when others had been rewarded) enhances the impact of the most recent attitude response.

An additional challenge to dissonance theory comes from Bem (e.g. 1967) in the form of self perception theory. Working from a behaviourist's view, Bem contested the assumption that attitudes may exist independently of observable behaviour, and suggested that attitudes are a person's own description of his likes and dislikes, and that these arise from observation of his own behaviour. Bem's example is the answer a person gives to the question, 'Do you like brown bread?' ... 'I must do; I'm always eating it.' Thus self perception theory claims that just as we observe other people's behaviour and infer their attitudes, so too we observe our own behaviour and infer our own attitudes.

Bem demonstrated support for his theory by repeating the forced compliance experiment of Festinger and Carlsmith (1959). The original experiment was simulated by having subjects listen to a tape recording which described a person who had participated in the boring task. The control subjects were asked to evaluate that person's attitude to the task, while the experimental subjects were told that the person had accepted an offer of one dollar (or twenty dollars in a different condition) to tell the next person that the task was interesting. Subjects were then asked to evaluate the person's attitude to the task. In Bem's experiment the twenty dollar condition did not differ from the control, but it did differ, as in the original experiment, from the one dollar condition, such that subjects who had observed a person being paid one dollar for the deception thought that person would have a more favourable attitude to the task, than did subjects who had observed a person being paid twenty dollars. Bem suggested that in the original Festinger and Carlsmith study subjects had observed their own behaviour and inferred their attitudes, just as in his simulation, his subjects had observed another person's behaviour and inferred his attitudes.

For several years the self perception interpretation challenged the dissonance interpretation, and various attempts (e.g. Taylor, 1975) were made to support one theory at the other's expense. Greenwald (1975) maintains that such attempts were inconclusive because they seldom ruled out an explanation in terms of the other theory. A more recent suggestion (Fazio, Zanna and Cooper, 1977) is that both theories can be applied, but to different areas of the attitude continuum: self perception theory being applicable to attitude congruent behaviour, that is, attitudinal positions which a subject finds acceptable, and dissonance theory being applicable to attitudinal positions with which the subject disagrees

Bem's self perception theory has been further developed into the area of attribution (e.g. Zanna and Cooper, 1976) which will be considered in the next chapter. However, the important point to be made in concluding a discussion on dissonance theory is that it started by being extremely influential, was heavily criticized and more recently returned in its influence but in a very different form. The more recent influence of dissonance theory has been the development of Nuttin's ideas of response contagion and Bem's self perception theory, leading to aspects of attribution. It is thus a good example of a theory which has modified itself in response to inconsistent information. In this process the original theory may have been exhausted. However, if the main function of a theory is to generate research and further knowledge about its phenomenon, then dissonance theory has served attitude research remarkably well.

5 Social judgment theories

A different group of attitude theories (e.g. Sherif and Hovland, 1961; Upshaw, 1962, 1965; Eiser and Stroebe, 1972) stresses, not the principle of consistency, but the idea that attitudes are *judgments*: that is, a person who has a particular attitude towards something, say a political party, has made a judgment of that party. This approach holds that, as social judgments, attitudes are similar to physical judgments and are in some ways subject to similar influences (see Eiser and Stroebe 1972 for a full discussion of this point). This section will attempt to show how the most successful of the social judgment theories, accentuation theory (e.g. Eiser and Stroebe, 1972), while still treating attitudes as judgments, also relies heavily on the principle of consistency.

The early work in social judgment was begun by Thurstone in 1928 and was concerned with attitude measurement. Thurstone believed that subjects with differing attitudes could rate the favourability of attitude statements and give the ratings without being influenced by their own attitudes. For example, one of Thurstone's studies (Thurstone and Chave, 1929) was concerned with attitudes towards the church, and one of his attitude statements was as follows:

> I think the Church is a hindrance to religion, for it still depends on magic, superstition and myth.

It was Thurstone's view that whatever their attitudes towards the church, different subjects would rate this statement similarly, when asked to assess its favourability to the church. This view was tested and upheld by Hinckley (1932) who asked subjects to rate a large number of statements about attitudes towards negroes on an eleven point scale ranging from extremely favourable to extremely unfavourable towards negroes. Hinckley used a 'carelessness criterion', such that subjects who gave the same rating to more than 30 per cent of the statements were eliminated from the analysis.

It was later suggested by Hovland and Sherif (1952) that Hinckley's support for Thurstone resulted from his failure to use subjects with differing attitudes, and that this failure was due to his use of the carelessness criterion. That is, Hovland and Sherif believed that Hinckley was actually eliminating subjects with extreme attitudes at either end of the scale, and only using the ratings from those with moderate attitudes. It was thus scarcely surprising that his analysis supported Thurstone. Hovland and Sherif went on to show that there is an inverse relationship between subjects' attitudes and their favourability ratings, so that the more favourable a subject's attitude towards the issue in question the more unfavourable ratings he makes, or the more attitudinal positions he describes as unfavourable.

(a) *Assimilation and contrast theory*

This early work was incorporated into the first social judgment theory of attitude organization and change by Sherif and Hovland (1961), as assimilation and contrast theory. This proposes that subjects given attitude statements, or views about an attitudinal issue, to judge for the statements' favourability use their own position, or attitude, as a standard against which the statements are related and compared. Those that they find acceptable are rated as nearer to their (i.e. the subject's) own position, than is the mean rating of that statement given by a large number of subjects of varying attitudes. In practice, this 'assimilation' effect – the rating of acceptable statements near to a subject's own position – can be demonstrated by obtaining a number of different attitude statements toward an issue; for example if the issue is the Common Market, then an investigator would obtain as many different statements about the Common Market as possible, including some from all parts of the attitude continuum so that, ideally, all views towards the Common Market are expressed. The investigator would then ask a large number of subjects, whom he believes will have widely differing attitudes, to rate these statements for favourability on a scale ranging from extremely favourable to extremely unfavourable to the Common Market. The mean rating for each statement, from all the subjects, is often termed the 'scale value' of that statement and represents the favourability of the statement towards the issue. Assimilation can then be demonstrated by asking a further group of subjects to rate the statements for favourability. Subjects who are pro Common Market will assimilate favourable statements; – that is they will rate them as more favourable than the corresponding scale values of the statements (see Figure 2.2).

Contrast may be similarly demonstrated. Pro Common Market subjects will find unfavourable statements unacceptable, and these will be contrasted:– that is, they will be rated further from the subjects' own position when compared with the scale values of the statements (see Figure 2.2).

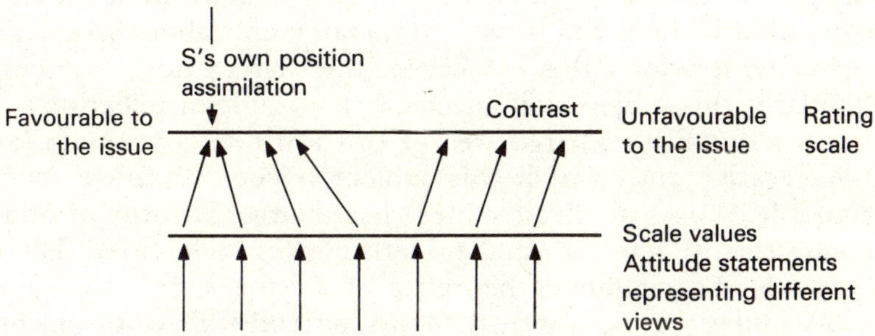

FIGURE 2.2 Assimilation and contrast theory: acceptable statements are assimilated towards S's own position. Unacceptable statements are contrasted

A pro Common Market subject, encountering a statement such as 'The EEC will eventually lead to economic, cultural and political unity' might judge this to be an extremely favourable view; that is he would assimilate it to his own view. However, the scale value of such a statement (determined from a number of subjects of differing attitudes) might be more neutral. An anti Common Market subject might interpret this statement as representing a relatively unfavourable view ('Who wants cultural unity with the Europeans, anyway?') and he would therefore assimilate it to his own position.

A further concept in the theory is that of involvement,

which in Sherif's studies (e.g. Sherif and Hovland, 1961; Sherif, Sherif and Nebergall, 1965) is generally taken to mean that the subject's attitude to the issue in question forms an important part of his self concept. In practice it often means that the subject is a member of a particular group or organization which has known attitudes to the issue. Involvement in an attitudinal issue affects what Sherif and Hovland term the 'latitudes of acceptance and rejection' – those areas of the attitude continuum which subjects find acceptable (and assimilate) and unacceptable (and contrast). An additional latitude of non-commitment was introduced by Sherif, Sherif and Nebergall. Involvement acts to vary the size of the latitudes of rejection and non-commitment, so that a subject who is very involved, for example in the issue of women's rights, will have a small latitude of non-commitment on this issue; that is there will be very few statements about women's rights with which this subject neither agrees nor disagrees. Similarly this subject will have a large latitude of rejection, so that there will be a large area of this attitude continuum (at the negative end) which this subject rejects, or finds unacceptable. A less involved subject has a larger latitude of non-commitment and a smaller latitude of rejection. Their latitudes of acceptance, theoretically, are the same.

Assimilation and contrast theory extends this work on the judgment of attitude statements to attitude change. It is reasonable to argue that attitude change often takes place by means of a persuasive communication, whether this is a pre-election message from a politician, something read in a newspaper, or an advertisement for cosmetics, and that this persuasive communication may be seen as an attitude statement, which can be judged in terms of its acceptability to the subject. However, assimilation and contrast theory runs into some difficulty at this point in that it now attempts to deal with changes in a subject's own position rather than changes in judged favourability of attitude statements. According to the theory, the persuasive communication, not the subject's own position (i.e. original attitude), now acts as the comparison against which other views are judged. If the communication is in the latitude of acceptance then it produces assimilation or a change in the subject's own position towards the communication (see Figure 2.3). It is not clear why the subject's own position should cease to act as the comparison in favour of the communication.

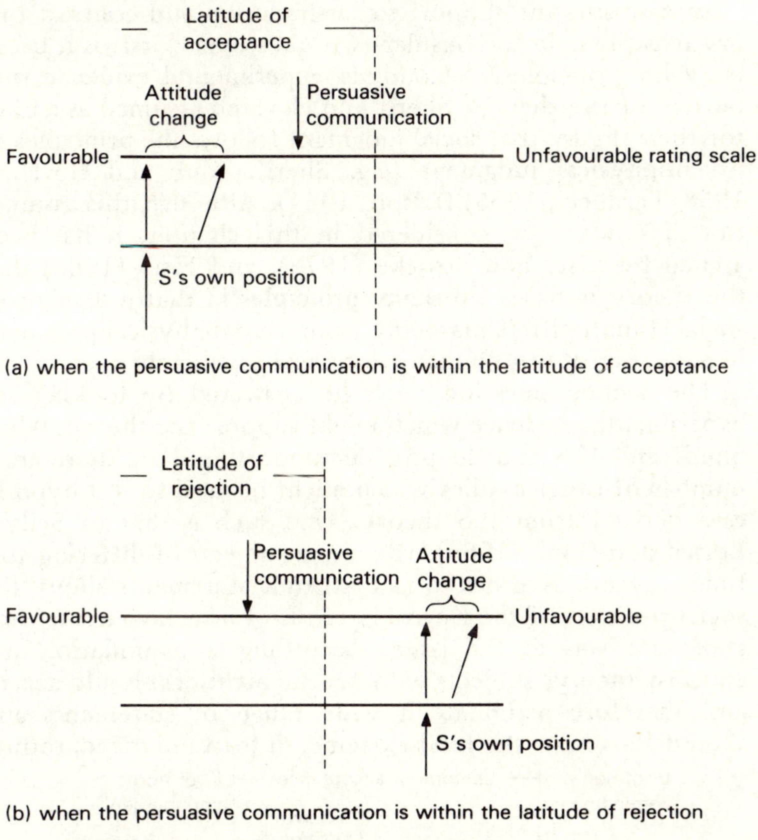

FIGURE 2.3 Attitude change according to assimilation and contrast theory

If the communication is in the latitude of rejection then, according to the theory, it will produce contrast. This contrast results in a 'boomerang effect' or change in the subject's attitude opposite to that intended by the communication. The reasoning behind this appears to be that since it is within the latitude of rejection and is acting as the comparison, the subject's own position will be contrasted from that comparison (see Figure 2.3). Again, there is no explanation of why the subject's own position ceases to be the comparison as in the initial part of the theory.

In assessing the support for assimilation and contrast theory it is possible to consider two questions. First, is it based on valid principles? Second, is experimental evidence supportive of the theory? Sherif and Hovland assumed as a basis for their theory that social judgment follows the principles of psychophysical judgment (e.g. Sherif, Taub and Hovland, 1958; Parducci, 1963; Helson, 1964). Although this assumption has not been considered in this chapter, it has been argued by Eiser and Stroebe (1972), and Eiser (1980) that the theory is based on shaky principles in that judgment of social stimuli differs markedly from psychophysical judgment in a number of ways which are critical for this theory.

The second question must be answered by looking for experimental evidence which might support the theory. While Sherif and Hovland do provide supporting data, there are a number of other studies which might be used to test hypotheses derived from the theory. One such is that of Selltiz, Edrich and Cook (1965) who asked subjects of differing attitudes towards Negroes to rate attitude statements about 'the social position of the Negro' in terms of how favourable each statement was to the issue. According to assimilation and contrast theory, subjects with neutral attitudes should accept and therefore assimilate a wide range of statements and should thus have the least extreme, or least polarized, ratings

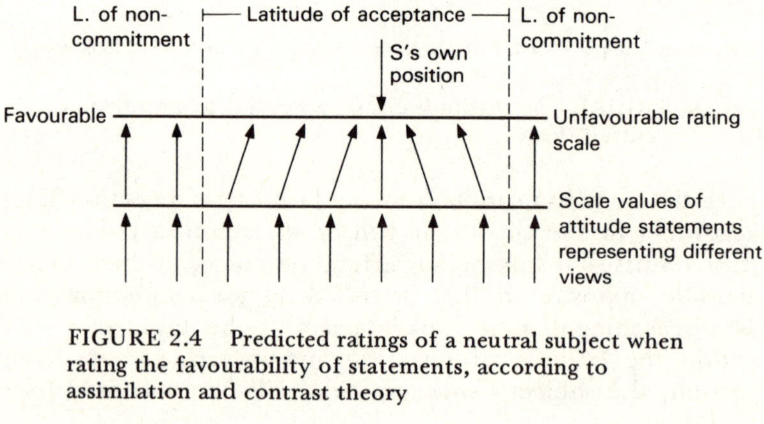

FIGURE 2.4 Predicted ratings of a neutral subject when rating the favourability of statements, according to assimilation and contrast theory

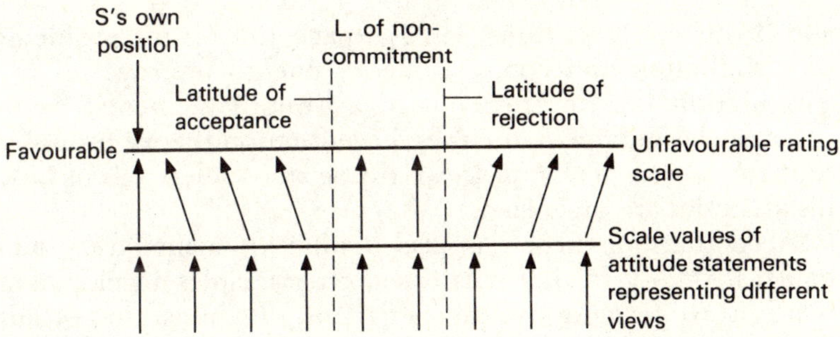

FIGURE 2.5 Predicted ratings of a favourable subject when rating the favourability of statements, according to assimilation and contrast theory

(see Figure 2.4). A subject whose attitude is at the favourable end of the continuum should assimilate favourable statements and contrast unfavourable statements, while a subject whose attitude is close to the unfavourable end should do the reverse. These latter subjects, though differing in attitude, should give the same degree of extremity in their overall judgments (see Figure 2.5).

In the Selltiz *et al.* experiment, and, indeed, in other similar studies (e.g. Eiser, 1971b; Upshaw, 1962; Zavalloni and Cook, 1965), these predicted results were not found. Instead, favourable subjects gave the most extreme ratings, as expected, but unfavourable subjects gave the least extreme, with neutral subjects taking a middle position. It is *not* possible to argue that the experiment did not really have any unfavourable subjects and so was not an adequate test of the theory, because a group of subjects with highly prejudiced attitudes, as indicated by an independent measure, was included. It is simply the case that assimilation and contrast theory cannot be supported by experimental data. In addition, it is based on untenable theoretical principles, and should therefore be abandoned.

(b) *Accentuation theory*

Accentuation theory has been developed by Eiser (e.g. Eiser

and Stroebe, 1972; Eiser, 1975) to account for the problems of assimilation and contrast theory and to improve on the formulation of the judgment of attitude statements. As in other social judgment theories, accentuation theory proposes that the way a person judges attitude statements tells us how his attitudes are organized.

Accentuation theory is also similar to assimilation and contrast theory in that it is based on principles developed in relation to psychophysical judgment, the most important being the principle of categorization or classification introduced by Tajfel (1959), and Tajfel and Wilkes (1963). According to this principle, if a series of stimuli which is labelled or classified (so that one part of the series is in one class, or has one label, and the other part is in another class, or has another label) then, when subjects come to judge the stimuli, their judgments show a shift which is in the direction of the class membership. Experimental evidence in support of this principle was provided by Tajfel and Wilkes, who asked subjects to judge the length of a series of lines. One group of subjects was led to expect that the short lines were labelled 'A' and the long lines labelled 'B', while another group was shown lines without labels. When subjects made their judgments, the group for whom the lines were labelled showed an accentuation of differences in length between the two categories of lines (category A and category B) as compared with the group who judged unlabelled lines. The effect of this so-called 'super-imposed classification' (i.e. the A and B labels) is an apparently simple and obvious principle. Nevertheless it is extremely important in social judgment, as well as psychophysical judgment, and has been applied to prejudice (e.g. Tajfel, Sheikh and Gardner, 1964; Tajfel, 1969) and to attitudes (e.g. Eiser, 1971a; Eiser and Mower White, 1975).

A major claim of accentuation theory is that attitude statements which a person is asked to judge can also be influenced by a superimposed classification. This was demonstrated by Eiser (1971b) in a study in which subjects rated attitude statements concerned with the non-medical use of drugs using a permissive–restrictive scale. In one condition of the study half of the statements (those which were most permissive) were labelled as originating from the *Gazette*, while the remainder (the restrictive statements) were labelled as originating from the *Messenger*. When the ratings from subjects in this condition were compared with those from subjects in a control condition in which no labels were used, it was shown that the labelling, or superimposed classification, caused more extreme judgments (see Figure 2.6).

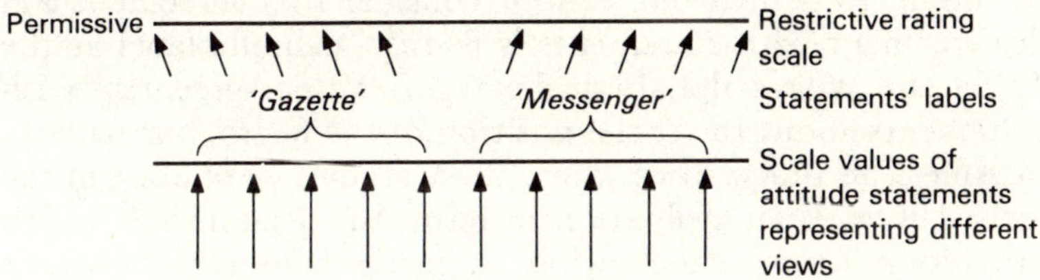

FIGURE 2.6 The effects of a superimposed classification on the judgment of attitude statements, as demonstrated by Eiser (1971b)

Thus it has been shown that it is possible that attitude statements can be subject to the effects of a superimposed classification. Accentuation theory further claims that a person's own agreement or disagreement can act as such a classification and cause a shift in judgment. This consideration provides a partial explanation of the Selltiz *et al.* results; that is, favourable, or pro-negro subjects, agreeing with those statements which were favourable towards negroes and disagreeing with statements which were unfavourable, thus used this agreement/disagreement classification as an additional cue in their judgment and so gave more extreme ratings than a more neutral judge (see Figure 2.7).

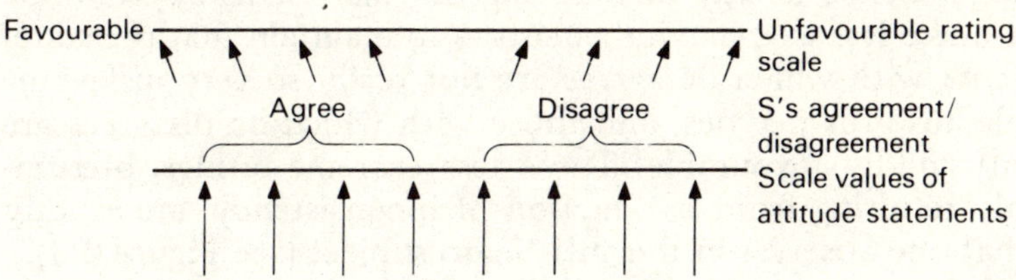

FIGURE 2.7 Agreement and disagreement acting as a superimposed classification in the judgment of attitude statements

A fuller explanation of the Selltiz *et al.* results, and those from similar studies (e.g. Upshaw, 1962; Zavalloni and Cook, 1965) requires one to consider the evaluative language in which the attitude rating scale is presented, and it is in this proposal that accentuation theory again differs from earlier theories, and makes a further substantial claim. If one takes the example of Selltiz's attitudinal issue – the social position of the negro – then one cannot consider that agreement and disagreement with statements is *merely* a simple label as the Tajfel and Wilkes alphabetical categories are. Agreement with statements about the social position of the negro, particularly in American universities where these studies were done in the early 1960s, is an evaluation in terms of social norms, which provide a strong expectation of being favourable towards negroes. Subjects are, quite simply, being asked to judge statements on value-laden dimensions, and the linguistic labels of the scale are a vital part of accentuation theory's explanation.

For the pro-negro subject, rating statements about the social position of the negro on a favourable–unfavourable to negroes scale, the task is comparatively simple: he can rate the statements with which he agrees near the evaluatively positive end of the scale, and those with which he disagrees near the evaluatively negative end of the scale, and he is making consistent judgments. The anti-negro subject has a more difficult task in that the statements with which he agrees are in effect nearer to the evaluatively negative (i.e. unfavourable) end of the scale, and those with which he disagrees nearer to the evaluatively positive (i.e. favourable) end of the scale. He is therefore being asked to make inconsistent judgments. One way of reducing this inconsistency would be to make less extreme judgments – to maintain that the statements with which he agrees are not really so very unfavourable towards negroes, and those with which he disagrees are only mildly favourable. These less extreme ratings, presumably resulting from a reduction of inconsistency, are exactly what one observes in the anti-Negro subject (see Figure 2.8).

An experiment demonstrating this explanation was reported by Eiser and Mower White (1974a). Teenage subjects were first given a measure of their attitudes to authority by being

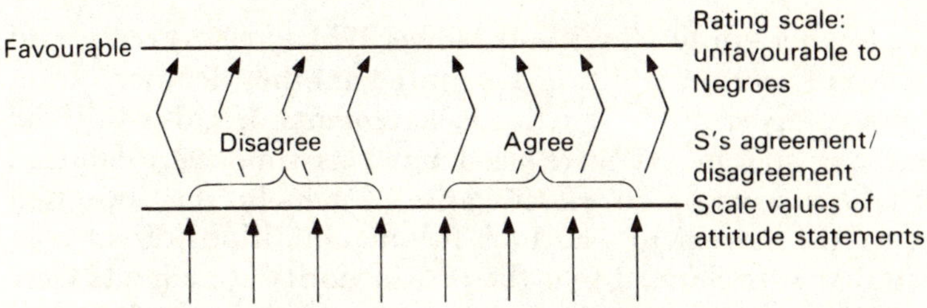

FIGURE 2.8 Reduction of inconsistency by an anti-Negro subject when rating statements on a scale on which the evaluatively positive end describes those with which he disagrees, and the evaluatively negative end describes those with which he agrees

asked to rate how much they agreed or disagreed with ten attitude statements, five being broadly pro-authority, and five broadly anti-authority. These were supposedly made by people of their own age when asked about adult authority, but were in fact statements longer than normally used in attitude studies (see Eiser and Stroebe, 1972, pp. 159-60 for the full text of the statements). Subjects were then asked to rate these statements on two types of scales. Type I was a group of five scales of which the pro-authority term was positively evaluative and the anti-authority term was negatively evaluative; (patient/impatient, level-headed/hot-headed, cooperative/uncooperative, obedient/disobedient, and well-mannered/ill-mannered). Type 2 was a group of five scales with the evaluations reversed: the anti-authority term was positively evaluated and the pro-authority term was negatively evaluated; (progressive/old-fashioned, unconventional/conventional, independent/dependent, imaginative/unimaginative, adventurous/unadventurous). Results showed that subjects give more extreme ratings when they can describe statements with which they agree in evaluatively positive terms, and those with which they disagree in evaluatively negative terms. Thus anti-authority subjects (as assessed by the initial attitude measure) gave more extreme ratings on Type 2 scales, than on Type 1 scales, whereas pro-authority subjects gave the reverse results, demonstrating that ratings were made so as to be consistent with the subject's agreement or disagreement with the statements.

A further study (Eiser and Mower White, 1975) replicated this result, and in addition attempted another demonstration of the categorization of attitude statements. In this study the same ten statements were used but this time were labelled with a superimposed classification – namely the supposed sex of the statement's author. In one condition (direct condition) it was claimed that the pro-authority statements were made by girls, and the anti-authority statements by boys, by printing a different girl's or boy's name under each statement. In a second condition (reverse condition) the claim was reversed: pro-authority statements were made by boys and anti-authority statements by girls. In a control condition no cue as to the statements' authors was given. In this study four Type 1 scales (the pro-authority term being positive) and four Type 2 scales (the anti-authority term being positive) were used. Half of each of these scale types were described as marked scales (e.g. bold/timid, polite/rude); the anti-authority term was seen as being more applicable to boys, and the pro-authority term was seen as being more applicable to girls, as described by the subjects of a pilot study. The remaining scales were unmarked (e.g. with it/old fashioned, helpful/unhelpful); neither term was seen as being more applicable to boys or girls. The terms of the marked scales were consistent with the superimposed classification in the direct condition but inconsistent in the reverse condition: subjects in the direct condition received pro-authority statements supposedly made by girls and could rate them on the marked scales as extremely pro-authority, since the pro-authority end of the scale was applicable to girls. Similarly anti-authority statements, made by boys, could be given an extreme rating since the anti-authority end of the scale was applicable to boys. It was therefore predicted that on the marked scales subjects in the direct condition should give more extreme ratings (i.e. consistent descriptions) than those in both the control and reverse conditions for whom a consistent description was not possible. On the unmarked scales, however, where there is no question of consistency or inconsistency with the superimposed classification, because the scales have no sex-linked connotations, subjects in both direct and reverse conditions should give more extreme ratings than control subjects as a result of the superimposed cue, or labelling of the statements with boys' or girls' names. Both predictions were confirmed.

Accentuation theory, and the experiments which support it (e.g. Eiser, 1971b; Eiser and Mower White, 1974a, 1975; Osmon and Mower White, 1977), have two major emphases. First, that attitude statements are subject to the effects of a superimposed classification, and second, that the evaluative connotations of the response scale are an important consideration. This latter point can be extended into a broader issue: that attitudes are closely linked to evaluative language. It follows from both the Eiser and Mower White studies discussed above, that a particular attitude which a person may hold determines his use of certain evaluative language, and thus one may infer a person's attitude by observing the types of evaluations he uses. For example, if one is describing a risky person, to call him 'fool-hardy' implies that one disapproves of him and his actions in question, whereas if he is 'adventurous' then one is demonstrating a favourable attitude towards him. In addition, Eiser (1975) suggests that the knowledge of a person's attitude may allow us to make an inference about his preferred way of thinking about the particular issue. Thus the pro-adult authority teenagers in the Eiser and Mower White studies may actually construe the issue of adult–child authority in terms of the values of politeness and obedience, whereas values such as boldness or independence may be less relevant to their conception of the issue.

If this is so, it may be that because certain values about an issue are held, then the consistent attitude develops. The implication here is that if subjects' value systems are influenced then their attitudes may be changed so as to be consistent with the value system. This was demonstrated by Eiser and Mower White (1974b), in an experiment in which three groups of teenage subjects were given an initial measure of their attitudes to adult authority. This was followed by a second similar measure, which the 'pro-bias' condition was told was designed to assess 'how polite, obedient, helpful and co-operative you are', whereas the 'anti-bias' condition was told that the second measure was to assess 'how bold, adventurous, creative and with-it you are'. A control condition was told that the second measure was a check on the initial measure. Compared to the control subjects, those in the pro-bias condition showed attitude change in a pro direction, and those in the anti-bias condition change in an anti direction, showing that making particular values relevant to subjects can cause attitudes to change so as to be consistent with those values.

A somewhat similar study by Eiser and Ross (1977) required subjects to use evaluative language by writing essays on capital punishment following an initial measure of attitudes to this issue. Subjects were asked to include as many as possible of a list of fifteen words, which in one condition were those which a supporter of capital punishment might use to describe the abolitionist view in negatively evaluative terms (e.g. irresponsible, over-idealistic). In a second condition the list of words were also negatively evaluative, but which an abolitionist might use to describe the pro capital punishment position (e.g. barbaric, callous, sadistic). There were no instructions as to whether the essays should support the abolitionist or the capital punishment position. A final attitude measure followed the essay writing. The results indicated that subjects in the first condition, who used negatively evaluative language implying the abolitionist view, shifted their attitudes in the direction of increased support for capital punishment, whereas those in the second condition who used words implying a negative evaluation of capital punishment became more opposed to the issue. It thus appears that actual use of particular evaluative language can direct attitudes so that they are consistent with that language.

Accentuation theory demonstrates, therefore, what Eiser (1975) calls a 'two-way process': the type of linguistic evaluations a person uses are dependent upon his attitude. In addition his attitude may be altered by his listening to, or his use of, evaluative language. This two-way process is perhaps most easily exemplified in a political speech. A politician describes the policies of his own party in positively evaluative language because, in accentuation theory terms, his attitude determines the type of language he uses. His speech is designed to change the attitudes of his audience to his way of thinking. In other words, his evaluative language is used so that his audience change their attitudes to be consistent to the evaluations they hear. Accentuation theory thus relies heavily on the notion of consistency, but is more complex than the original consistency theory put forward by Heider (1946, 1958). Balance theory deals with fairly restricted situations and is limited, at least in Heider's proposals, to two or three entities. Accentuation theory, while still using Heider's basic idea, relates attitudes far more broadly to a person's values and the social influences prevalent in society.

6 Attitudes and behaviour

As was stated at the beginning of this chapter, social psychology has devoted a great deal of effort to the study of attitudes. Presumably this is not a totally academic exercise. There must, after all, be many instances when knowledge of a person's attitudes allows his behaviour to be predicted. Indeed, there is a general assumption, both among psychologists and laymen, that attitudes and behaviour should be, and are, consistent. The function of a pre-election political speech, although ostensibly to change the attitudes of the electorate, is really to ensure that voting behaviour is consistent with that attitude. An advertiser does not really mind whether you like his product, but he assumes that if he can make you like it, you will buy it. Social psychologists have, however, been concerned about the so-called attitude-behaviour discrepancy for many years; the assumption of consistency is seldom realized in psychological experiments.

For example, La Piere (1934), in probably the best known study in this field, reported his visits to 250 hotels and restaurants in the United States while accompanied by a Chinese couple. They were refused service once, but in many were 'treated with ... more than ordinary consideration' (p.232). While the behaviour towards these Chinese visitors appeared favourable, the attitudes expressed on a questionnaire sent later to the proprietors of the same establishments were not, 92 per cent saying that they would *not* accept Chinese guests.

Wicker (1969) reviewed a number of studies in this area and suggested that the total evidence indicated that it is most likely that attitudes are unrelated rather than closely related to behaviour. This somewhat sober conclusion leads to a number of questions. For example, is this an aspect of social psychology in which inconsistency rather than consistency is prevalent? Throughout this book there is an attempt to show that consistency is a cornerstone to social behaviour in that it provides a basis for prediction of that behaviour. The attitude-behaviour discrepancy is, at first sight, a little embarrassing for this view, because one cannot predict behaviour on the basis of inconsistency, there being nothing to base the prediction on. It is therefore important to investigate this discrepancy in an effort to find possible reasons for it.

One cause of the attitude-behaviour discrepancy may lie in the possibility that the behaviour in question is perhaps related to a number of attitudes, only one of which may be investigated by the social psychologist. For example, a person who believes in a boycott of South African produce may, or may not, buy South African apples depending on other relevant attitudes: he may also believe that one should buy the best quality fruit available, or he may wish to please his wife whom he knows likes those particular apples. If social psychologists have inquired into the relevance of only one attitude to behaviour then they may well be rewarded with inconsistency. Just as it is naive to expect consideration of one single attitude to allow prediction of behaviour, the reverse also applies: there can be various behaviours that are relevant to a particular attitude; for example, a prejudiced attitude can manifest itself in a variety of behaviours, perhaps only one of which is investigated.

Related to this cause of the discrepancy is a further one: social norms provide us with ideas about 'proper' behaviour under certain conditions and there may be instances in which we cannot defy those norms to make our behaviour consistent with our attitudes. For example in La Piere's study the norm of being polite to guests may have overridden consistency and turning those guests away.

According to Deutsch (1949) a further reason is that

people may not know how to behave in a way that is consistent with their attitudes. While this seems unlikely to be so in many cases it may be that, for example, a person may like another, but at the same time may not know how to initiate friendly behaviour.

Finally, an important reason for the attitude-behaviour discrepancy has been pointed out by Eiser (1980), who claims that most of the studies in the area have investigated relatively specific behaviours and attempted to relate them to far more general attitudes. Using the La Piere study to illustrate this point, it is apparent that the questionnaire sent to restaurant and hotel proprietors assessed general attitudes towards 'members of the Chinese race' without mention of any specific factors involved in the situation when the behavioural assessment was made: the particular Chinese couple were probably well-behaved and well-dressed, were accompanied by a non-Chinese American, and scarcely conformed to the stereotyped Chinese. The behavioural assessment therefore was far more specific than was the attitudinal assessment, and far from expecting consistency, one might be surprised to find it.

A similar way of describing the attitude-behaviour discrepancy has been put forward by Fishbein (1967) who questions the assumption of consistency between behaviour and attitudes. Fishbein's model proposes that behaviour is best predicted, not by attitudes, but by behavioural intentions (BI) which, in turn, are a joint function of the person's attitude towards performing the behaviour in question (A. act), his beliefs about what other people expect him to do (NB), and his motivation to comply (MC) with these expectations or norms. Fishbein has expressed his model mathematically as follows:

$$\text{Behaviour (B)} \sim \text{BI} = (\text{A.act}) \times w_0 + (\text{NB} \times \text{MC})\, w_1$$

It appears from the model that the two main contributors to behavioural intentions – the attitude to the particular behaviour and the product of normative beliefs and motivation to comply with them can each be weighed (w_0 and w_1) depending on the type of behaviour being predicted and the conditions under which the behaviour is performed.

A number of studies have given support to Fishbein's model (e.g. Ajzen and Fishbein, 1972; Fishbein and Ajzen, 1975) whereas more recently Songer-Nocks (1976) has suggested that it may be too simple to account for all situational variables by the weighting system. It may be, therefore, that the model should be revised. However, its main point in this discussion is to show that attitude measurement must be more specific, maybe in terms of the attitude toward the particular behaviour under consideration – if social psychology is to demonstrate attitude-behaviour consistency.

7 Conclusion

This chapter has discussed how attitudes that a person holds are consistent with each other and with his values. Many attitude theorists have utilized the principle of consistency in elaborating their ideas. Where this has not been the case (e.g. Sherif and Hovland, 1961) the theory has not been supported either in empirical research, or in the principles on which it is based. In general, experimental support for consistency theories, and for accentuation theory (Eiser, 1975), has been good, although that for balance theory (Heider, 1953) is limited to fairly specific conditions. In addition, there are biases, other than balance (or consistency) which are influential in the simple POX structure with which balance theory deals. Dissonance theory (Festinger, 1957) might be described as having outlived its usefulness in that the original theory has been abandoned in favour of the more limited self perception theory (Bem, 1967) and Nuttin's (1975) views concerning response contagion. The more recent accentuation theory has combined ideas of consistency with those of social judgment and provides a useful approach which describes the consistency of attitudes with the values of the person who holds them and the evaluative language in which they are expressed. Finally, this chapter dealt with the problem of the attitude-behaviour discrepancy, and its possible causes. It appears important that the relevant, and probably specific, attitude is considered if consistency is to be found.

It is perhaps interesting to consider here, on a broader level, why there is a general assumption of consistency between attitudes and behaviour if it is so rarely found in experimental practice. It has been pointed out that psychologists must be aware that the attitudes they measure must be sufficiently specific for the behaviour in question, and that other relevant attitudes can be important. It would seem unlikely that the layman's assumption of consistency could be totally wrong, for it is presumably based on observation and experience which has become generalized into this assumption. The same may apply to consistency between attitudes: we have observed it in the past and therefore believe it to be so. It is no doubt convenient to have this general rule of consistency between attitudes, and attitudes and behaviour because it acts to simplify cognitive representations of social interactions and to allow their prediction. However, this convenience would soon be forfeited if it had no basis in reality, as the prediction of social interaction would cease to be accurate. It may therefore be more realistic to look for problems with experiments which do not demonstrate consistency among attitudes and behaviour, rather than to question the assumption of consistency.

3 The attribution of behaviour

I Introduction

As has been stressed in earlier chapters our social interactions with other people are highly dependent on our being able to predict their behaviour. In many ways such predictions are based on previous observation and description of their behaviour, the description often being in terms of trait words. To give an indication of the importance of these words in our language, Allport and Odbert (1936) counted 18,000 traits in a standard English dictionary, of which 4,504 described 'consistent and stable modes of an individual's adjustment to his environment' (Allport, 1937, p.306). Such a vocabulary supports the view that the describing of people is an extremely important use of language, and must be a vital part of social behaviour.

Social psychology has dealt with interpersonal description in a number of ways. The first of these is as 'impression formation' or 'person perception', the main body of work stemming from the classic experiment of Asch (1946) on central and peripheral traits, and how separate traits are united to form a composite inference (e.g. Anderson, 1962, 1965; Triandis and Fishbein, 1963; Wishner, 1960). A second concerns attribution theory, which deals with the way we find causes for events, and principally how we attribute causes to the behaviour of other people and ourselves. It is the latter with which this chapter is concerned.

As already mentioned, interpersonal description is usually in terms of trait words, but when we say someone is, for example, 'opinionated' or 'industrious' we are doing something psychologically very different from describing his personality. Indeed, many present-day psychologists interested in personality theory would seriously question the validity of traits as adequate for describing personality (e.g. Bowers, 1973; Endler, 1973; Hampson, 1982; Mischel, 1968, 1973). Traits are used by the layman firstly as descriptions of behaviour, and secondly (and more importantly for attribution theory) as labels for the cause and evaluation of that behaviour. Thus to say 'Harry is studious' is shorthand for describing Harry's behaviours which we choose to label in this way; for saying that Harry, rather than the particular situation he is in, is the cause of this behaviour; and further, that we approve of this behaviour; if we were to disapprove Harry would be said to be 'a swot'.

In discussing attribution theory, this chapter will first consider the basic statements relating to the topic, made by various psychologists (e.g. Heider, 1958; Jones and Davis, 1965; Kelley, 1967). The major concern here has been the conditions under which the cause of behaviour is thought to be the person – his ability, personality, or effort – or else the situation he is in. This concern is echoed throughout attribution theory, as will be seen in the following section: that on self attributions. The idea that we need to attribute our own behaviour (i.e. to explain to ourselves why we did what we did), rather than having immediate knowledge of our feelings, characteristics and attitudes can be a little disturbing; nevertheless, if one believes this aspect of attribution theory, then it can throw some intriguing light on one's behaviour. One of the ways in which this aspect of social psychology has attempted to be concerned with applied fields is in the attribution of success and failure. It is apparent that how one attributes the cause of successful behaviour – whether to oneself or to the situation in which it occurred – may markedly affect similar future behaviour. In the same way the attribution of another person's successes or failures to himself, or to luck, or to environmental causes may affect his future behaviour. This has been introduced into both clinical and educational fields with some advantage, as will be discussed later in the chapter.

A final aspect of attribution which will be considered is relevant to all earlier discussions. It appears that an attribution, once made, is seldom abandoned or changed. This so-called 'primacy effect' and its implications will be outlined at the end of the chapter. In conclusion, there will be a consideration of the functions of attribution, in terms of evaluation and consistency, and an analogy will be drawn between a layman's attributions and those of the professional psychologist.

2 Basic statements in attribution theory

The major concern in attribution theory has been the conditions under which behaviour is attributed to the person as opposed to the situation in which he behaves. The early work introducing this topic was by Heider (1944, 1958) who claimed that people attempt to see the social environment as predictable and therefore controllable. In order to predict the behaviour of another, we look for the conditions which will explain it, such as his ability or his assumed personality, which Heider termed 'personal causes' (1958, p.16). Alternatively his behaviour may be attributed to 'impersonal causes' such as a different person, or some non-personal event. If behaviour is seen as being controlled by these external or impersonal causes, then attributions in terms of personality traits are less likely to be made. We would be unlikely to describe somebody as 'opinionated' if we observe him in a debating chamber, particularly if we know that outside the debate he holds opposite views. His behaviour is more likely to be ascribed to the situation he is in. Heider (1958) claims that the effect of the situation is very rarely fully considered by the layman as the cause of behaviour, because we are biased towards making personal attributions. It is interesting that a similar claim has been made by Mischel (1968) with respect to the way personality theorists have considered the causes of behaviour suggesting that both laymen and psychologists alike have some bias towards making personal attributions.

In addition to distinguishing between personal and impersonal attributions, Heider stresses that 'intention is the central factor in personal causality' (1958, p.102). Thus cases of personal causality are only appropriate when the actor intended to behave in a particular way, and did so, Heider's views, and especially those of intentionality, have been elaborated by Jones and Davis (1965) whose model has been influential in the attribution literature. It assumes that the perceiver observes the overt behaviour of the actor; decides whether the actor knew that his behaviour would have the outcomes produced, and whether the actor intended those outcomes. When the perceiver describes the behaviour and the actor's personality in the same way, then he is said to have made a 'correspondent inference'. For example if the perceiver observes placid behaviour in the actor, a correspondent inference would be made if it is assumed that this reflects an intention to be placid, which in turn reflects a placid disposition. This notion is, of course, consistency under a different name: a consistent attribution might be said to be made when the actor's personality and intentions are seen as directly resulting in characteristic behaviour. The attribution that an actor's behaviour is a result of the situation does not allow such consistent inferences between behaviour and personality, and it is therefore not surprising that Heider suggested that there is a bias towards personal attributions; it is these that are most consistent.

According to the model of Jones and Davis the extent to which an actor's behaviour is attributed to his personality and intentions varies with the number of non-common effects of the behaviour, and the social desirability of the effects. Thus correspondent inferences are more likely if the observed behaviour results in a large number of consequences which would not have been produced if the actor's personality or intentions had been different. In addition, behaviour which is socially desirable tells the observer little about the actor's personality, whereas unusual or deviant behaviour is more informative; one would infer more about the personal characteristics of a Sunday afternoon balloonist than about an individual who spends his evenings drinking in the pub.

A study by Jones, Worchel, Goethals and Grumet (1971) illustrates this point. Subjects were asked to read essays which had supposedly been written by others who had taken a popular or unpopular stand towards the legalization of the sale of marijuana. In addition, they were given information either that the writer had been asked to take this stand, or that he had been given a free choice over the position advocated. Subjects were then asked to estimate the writer's true opinion. In accordance with the Jones and Davis predictions, an essay advocating an unpopular position, when written under choice conditions, was seen as more representative of the writer's opinion than was a more popular stand.

While in some respects the model proposed by Jones and Davis accords with common sense, perhaps because common sense engages in attributions in the way the model suggests, there are certain problems. Eiser (1979, 1980) has pointed out that the idea that personality causes intentions which in turn cause behaviour is fraught with difficulties. Any socially undesirable behaviour is rarely intentional, even though it *may* be the result of a socially undesirable personality trait: one does not suppose that careless people intend to behave carelessly, nor that they intend the consequences of this behaviour.

A further important statement on attribution theory comes from Kelley (1967) who proposes that four criteria are used to decide whether behaviour is attributable to personal or external causes. The first criterion, distinctiveness, is perhaps the most important. If the perceiver describes a person as 'pompous' we can only accept this attribution if we know that there are other people whom this perceiver will not describe in this way. Distinctiveness also plays a part in attributions of socially normative behaviour: if many people behave in a particular way in a situation then one cannot make personal attributions with any certainty. Conversely, for example, if one knows that a person habitually keeps a crocodile in his bath one might plausibly refer to him as 'animal-loving', 'dirty' or 'eccentric', but one would not, presumably, ascribe this behaviour to the situation.

Kelley's second criterion, consensus, suggests that a person's behaviour is more likely to be thought due to personal causes if a number of different perceivers make that particular attribution. The remaining criteria are consistency over time, and consistency over modality. Thus if repeated observation of a person's behaviour leads to the same attribution then it is likely that the behaviour is the result of personal rather than situational causes. Similarly, personal attributions will only result if the person is consistent across different situations. For example, if he is always timid then this may be seen as his personal attribute, but if he is adventurous in some respects and timid in others then there will be a tendency to look for some external condition which corresponds to the changes in his behaviour.

Kelley's criteria have been tested in an experiment by McArthur (1972). Subjects read statements describing the behaviour of a particular person in the presence of a particular stimulus (e.g. 'John laughs at the comedian'). Further information was given relating to distinctiveness (e.g. 'John also laughs (vs. does not laugh) at almost every other comedian'); consensus (e.g. 'Almost everyone (vs. hardly anyone) who hears the comedian laughs at him'); and consistency over time (e.g. 'In the past John has almost always (vs. never) laughed at the same comedian'). Subjects rated the probability, in each case, that the behaviour (i.e. John's laughing) was due to the person described (e.g. John); the stimulus (e.g. the comedian); or the particular circumstances.

Personal attributions were most frequent, as predicted by Kelley, when distinctiveness and consensus were low and consistency high. For example, 'John laughs at the comedian; hardly anyone who hears the comedian laughs at him; John also laughs at almost every other comedian; in the past John has almost always laughed at the same comedian'. Stimulus attributions were most frequent under conditions of high distinctiveness, high consensus and high consistency. The particular circumstances were seen as being responsible when distinctiveness was high, and consensus and consistency low. In addition, a fairly frequent attribution was that the behaviour was due to a combination of person and stimulus, particularly under conditions of low distinctiveness, and high consensus and consistency, or alternatively, high distinctiveness and consistency and low consensus.

3 Self attributions

(a) *External information as a source of self attribution*

Much of the intriguing work in attribution theory has concerned how we infer and describe our own feelings, emotions, attitudes and characteristics. On first consideration it may seem strange that we do not immediately know our feelings and attitudes, but some authors have argued that indeed we do not, and that self descriptions require observation of our own behaviour. It is also the case that much of the work contrasting self description with the description of others has thrown new light on the way attributions are made, and the reasons why we engage in this very commonplace but apparently non-obvious behaviour.

One of the earliest studies used to show that self attribution is not as obvious as it might seem initially is that of Schachter and Singer (1962), who told subjects that they were investigating the effects of the compound 'suproxin' on vision. Subjects were, in fact, injected with epinephrine, a drug producing heightened physiological arousal. One group was informed of the effects of the drug, while another was not. A third group received a placebo injection. Cross-cutting this manipulation, subjects were then exposed to a confederate who, in one condition, behaved in a euphoric manner, building and flying paper aeroplanes, and practising basketball shots, while in the other condition the confederate behaved angrily, refusing to answer irritating questionnaire items. After witnessing the confederate's behaviour, subjects indicated their own mood on a questionnaire. It was expected that those who had been informed of the effects of the drug would attribute their heightened arousal to the injection they had received, and be unaffected by the confederate's behaviour. Those who were ignorant of the drug's effects were expected to label their arousal in accordance with the confederate's actions: happiness when he was euphoric, and anger when he was angry. The results supported these predictions, showing that physiological arousal for which a subject has no ready explanation may be interpreted in terms of external cues; thus our emotions may be labelled according to the characteristics of the situation.

A somewhat similar conclusion can be drawn from an experiment by Valins (1966). In this study male subjects were shown pictures of female nudes taken from *Playboy* magazine while at the same time listening to sounds which they were led to believe were their own amplified heart beats. The heart beats were in fact prerecorded so that they changed on a random half of the slides, and remained constant on the other half. Valins predicted that subjects' perceptions of their liking the pictures would be influenced by external information that suggested that they reacted more strongly to some than to others. Subjects did, in fact, judge those nudes that had apparently produced a change in heart rate as more attractive, suggesting that in determining how we feel about stimuli, we may pay particular attention to external rather than internal information. A further study by Valins (1972) indicated that, even when subjects were given the full details of the experimental procedure, the preferences persisted, a result which was interpreted as implying that they paid closer attention to pictures apparently producing a heart beat change in order to discover what was special about them.

Further work has concerned self attribution of motivation for particular behaviour. If certain actions are seen as being intrinsically rewarding then a person can conclude that because he enjoys this behaviour for its own sake, he must be a certain sort of person. Thus a person who enjoys playing tennis, may describe himself as 'athletic' or 'a sportsman'. However this description would be impossible if he sees his behaviour as being determined by extrinsic rewards such as the prize money or even the glory of winning the game. Thus we acknowledge a difference between playing a game to win and playing for the sake of playing. This aspect of self attribution has been investigated experimentally, for example, by Lepper, Greene and Nisbett (1973). In this study three groups of nursery-school children were asked to draw a picture. The 'expected reward' group were told that they would be given a certificate with ribbons and a gold seal as a reward for their picture, while the 'unexpected reward' group and the control group were not given this information. When the pictures were drawn, all children were praised, and the expected and unexpected reward groups received certificates. In a later session the children were able to choose drawing out of a number of other activities, and, as predicted, children in the expected reward group chose drawing less frequently than those in other groups. This result was interpreted in terms of extrinsic rewards; children in the expected reward group saw drawing as something to be done in order to receive a reward; when this was not promised, they did not draw. Other children could explain their previous drawing in terms of intrinsic rewards, 'I'm the kind of person who enjoys drawing', and would thus tend to choose this activity on another occasion.

(b) *Self perception theory*

An important aspect of self attribution has developed from Bem's (1967) proposition that we learn about our own attitudes and dispositions from observing our behaviour, in the same way that we learn about other people's attitudes and dispositions by observation of their behaviour. According to Bem, we infer that our attitudes and characteristics are consistent with the behaviour we emit and observe. While Bem's hypothesis may seem strange and in opposition to much of the earlier attitude theory literature (e.g. Festinger, 1957), experimental data can offer it a reasonable amount of support (e.g. Bandler, Madaras and Bem, 1968; Bem, 1965; 1967; Davison and Valins, 1969; Kiesler, Nisbett and Zanna, 1969; Ross, Insko and Ross, 1971). Bandler *et al.*, for example, gave subjects a series of thirty electric shocks. Ten of the shocks were preceded by a light which told subjects that they could escape the shocks by pressing a button. Subjects were also told that the experimenter would prefer them to escape from the shock, even though it might not be painful; these instructions were designed to allow subjects to interpret their escape as of their own choosing and hence that the shocks were indeed painful. In a further condition, identical shocks were given to the same subjects, the preceding light merely signalled a reaction time trial. In comparison, shocks in the first condition were rated as more painful than those in the reaction time condition. Thus it was concluded that subjects had inferred their attitudes to the shocks from observing their escape behaviour. However, a third condition did not support this conclusion. The remaining ten shocks were preceded by a light which indicated that the experimenter wanted the subject not to escape from the shock, even though they could do so by pressing a button. As in the first condition, most subjects complied with the experimenter's request and this time endured the shocks. It was predicted that enduring the shocks would be interpreted as self induced, and that they should therefore be seen as less painful. However shocks in this third condition were not rated differently from those in the reaction time condition.

Nisbett and Valins (1971) suggest that the failure of this experiment's third condition to support Bem's proposition may have resulted from requests to perform counter attitudinal behaviour (i.e. to endure the shocks) being seen as more controlling than requests to perform pro-attitudinal behaviour (to escape from the shocks). If subjects perceive that their behaviour is under external control then they may be less willing to infer their attitudes from it.

Even though experimental data and particularly that on autonomic behaviour (e.g. Nisbett and Schachter, 1966; Schachter and Singer, 1962), have supported Bem, the proposition is dependent on two assumptions. First, that we do not have independent or fixed knowledge of our attitudes, and second that we do not have direct knowledge of the causes of our behaviour. It thus appears that a person who is observing his behaviour and inferring his characteristics from this observation must, if Bem is correct, have some uncertainty about the causes of his behaviour and his related characteristics and attitudes. Nisbett and Valins (1971) have suggested that a brief sample of behaviour may not give sufficient information to allow an inference about personal characteristics which can be regarded with much confidence. Such an inference may therefore be more like a hypothesis, and may require an opportunity for testing. An experiment by Valins and Ray (1967) using snake-phobic subjects may illustrate this testing of the inference: subjects were shown pictures of snakes displayed on slides. Interspersed among the slides there were additional slides giving the word 'shock', and following the shock slides subjects received a mild electric shock through their fingers. While viewing the slides subjects listened to a prerecorded tape which they believed to be their own heart rate, but which was in fact designed so that the 'heart rate' increased at the shock slides but not at the snake slides. It was intended that subjects should infer that since they were more aroused following the shock slides than following the snake slides (due to the heart rate), they must be afraid of shocks but not afraid of snakes. An unusual, but appropriate, dependent measure was used in this experiment: the distance to which subjects could approach a thirty-inch boa constrictor. As predicted, phobic subjects were able to approach more closely than control subjects who had undergone the same procedure but were not led to believe that the sounds were made by their heartbeats. However, *before* approaching the snake, subjects were asked to report on their fear of snakes, and the experimental and control groups did not differ. Nisbett and Valins suggest that the heart rate feed back may have led to the hypothesis: 'Maybe I'm not as afraid of snakes as I thought.' This hypothesis would require testing (i.e. approaching a snake) before self description (or report) was altered.

(c) *Actor–observer differences*

Bem's work on self attribution, as well as that supporting it, assumes that we observe our own behaviour and infer our characteristics from it *in the same way* as we observe other people's behaviour and make inferences about their dispositions, attitudes and beliefs. However, a rather different suggestion has been made by Jones and Nisbett (1971), who compare the different (in their view) processes by which self and other attributions are made. According to these authors, a person attributes his own behaviour to situational causes, whereas when viewing another person's behaviour we very often attribute it to the dispositions or personality characteristics of others.

While a number of early studies, (e.g. Jones and Harris, 1967; Jones, Rock, Shaver, Goethals and Ward, 1968; McArthur, 1972), have been interpreted according to the Jones and Nisbett proposition, a study reported by Nisbett, Caputo, Legant and Maracek (1973) tested it in situations where equivalent forms of information were available to both the actor perceiving his own behaviour, and the observer perceiving another's behaviour. Student subjects were asked to write statements saying why they had chosen their major field of study and why they liked their girl friends. They were also asked to write a similar paragraph saying why their friend had made his choice of study and of girl friend. When answering for themselves, subjects were more likely to make situational or stimulus attributions ('She's a very warm person'). When describing their friend's choice subjects were more likely to make personal or dispositional attributions ('He likes blondes').

Jones and Nisbett claim that the difference in attributions made by actors and observers is due to different aspects of the available information being salient. When observing one's own behaviour one is more likely to focus attention on environmental cues that evoke this behaviour rather than the behaviour itself. Since an actor's attention is thus directed to the situation it is likely that he will attribute his behaviour as a response to the situation. For the observer, it is the other person's behaviour which claims most attention, and it is thus more likely to be thought due to dispositional rather than situational determinants. In addition, it has been pointed out by Mischel (1973) that a person sees his own behaviour in most situations in which he behaves and thus knows more about the variety of his own behaviour than does an observer. If, as Mischel argues, behaviour *is* primarily determined by the situation, the variations in an actor's behaviour will correspond to the variations in the situational determinants, and this correspondence will be noted by the actor.

It can therefore be argued that these actor–observer differences are dependent upon physical constraints: actors and observers have different perspectives, and different aspects such as situational cues or the behaviour being observed become the focus of attention. Storms (1973) devised a technique to overcome these physical constraints. Two-person conversations were video-taped by two separate cameras so that the participants' interactions were recorded from each of their perspectives. When the actor was able to view his own behaviour from what had been the observer's (i.e. the other person's) orientation, he became more internal or dispositional in his attributions to himself. When the reverse occurred – that is, when the observer viewed the conversation from what had been the actor's orientation – then attributions were more situational. These results suggest, as do Jones and Nisbett, that there is nothing particular about self attributions themselves which provide actor–observer differences. It is merely that the actor and observer have different perspectives on the behaviour being considered.

In concluding this section on self attributions it is apparent that a number of processes may be at work. First, it seems that we take cues from external sources – whether it be from others in a similar situation or from behaviour which is extrinsically rewarded – to infer our own characteristics. Second, and in a rather similar vein, Bem's self perception theory suggests that we may observe our own behaviour and from it make an inference about our characteristics, attitudes and dispositions. As already discussed, this theory can only hold so long as we are considering behaviour whose cause we do not know, and dealing with personal characteristics about which we are unsure. If I have a certain and long-standing dislike of cats, I would be unlikely to observe a cat purring on my knees and infer that perhaps they are not so bad after all. More probably, I should ascribe this behaviour (if it occurred at all), to my politeness at not wishing to offend my hostess whose cat I am suffering. However, if this experience is a new one for me, then it may be that Bem is correct. From observing my behaviour, I could indeed infer that I do like cats.

The final aspect of self attribution that was discussed was the elaboration by Jones and Nisbett of actor–observer differences. According to their view we attribute our own behaviour to situational causes, whereas other people's behaviour is ascribed to personal characteristics. At first sight this appears to contradict Bem's proposal that we infer our own characteristics in the same way as we do for others – by observing behaviour. The problem can possibly be explained by emphasizing that Bem's theory can only apply when we do not know how the behaviour is caused, and when it may be linked to personal characteristics of which we are uncertain. Actor–observer differences, on the other hand, probably result from different aspects of information, the behaviour or the situation, being salient for an observer and an actor respectively. The proposed processes at work in self attribution do not, therefore, contradict each other: according to Jones and Nisbett a person observes the situation he is in to explain his behaviour, but surely he will not do this if he is uncertain whether, and if so how, his behaviour may be linked to his personal characteristics. In these cases, it is more likely that Bem's proposition will hold, since these are the conditions under which his views seem most sensible.

4 Attribution of success and failure

One of the more important ways in which attribution theory has been introduced into applied fields is in the attribution of success and failure. It is apparent that many achievements must be affected by the way in which people ascribe their own successes and failures: a person is unlikely to continue to strive towards a goal if he attributes his failures to an enduring personal characteristic. Similarly if success is attributed to luck, or some situational factor, then future behaviour may also be affected. This aspect of attribution has centred round clinical psychology and educational problems, both of which will be discussed briefly later in this section. First, however, work relating to self attribution of success and failure will be considered.

(a) *Self attribution of success and failure*

Much of the work in this area has involved the personality dimension elaborated by Rotter (1966), internal-external locus of control. A detailed account of this would be out of place here, but some description is required. Briefly, as a result of work on social learning theory (Rotter, 1954), locus of control was outlined as a dimension which at the two extremes differentiates individuals who interpret the reinforcements they receive as contingent upon their own action, from those who believe that the reinforcements they receive are the result of luck, fate or unpredictable factors. The former individuals Rotter termed 'internals', those who have a belief in internal control of rewards, while the latter are said to be 'externals', having a belief in external control of rewards.

This dimension was used by Phares, Wilson and Klyver (1971), who asked subjects to perform four tasks described as measures of intellectual ability. Subjects were failed on two of the tasks, half the subjects failing under distracting conditions (the experimenters talking loudly to each other while subjects were attempting the task), while the remaining half failed under non-distracting conditions. Subjects were then given questionnaires asking about the adequacy of the experiment, the physical setting, and the subject's current mental and physical state. Under non-distracting conditions external subjects were more likely to attribute responsibility for failure to situational conditions, a result which was interpreted as defensive behaviour in externals, providing a way of reducing the negative consequences of failure. Under the distracting conditions there were no differences between internal and external subjects in attribution of blame for failure.

The locus of control dimension has been incorporated into a model of attribution of success and failure by Weiner, Frieze, Kukla, Reed, Rest and Rosenbaum (1971). These authors propose that four factors are used to predict and interpret the outcome of an event which may lead to success or failure: ability, effort, task difficulty and luck. While two of these components, ability and effort, are personal descriptions, the remaining two describe environmental factors, and this division of components corresponds to the internal-external locus of control dimension. However, an equally important dimension, according to Weiner *et al.*, is that of stability vs. instability: ability and task difficulty are seen as stable, enduring characteristics, whereas effort and luck are relatively variable. The authors outline the conditions under which the outcome of an event may be attributed to each of the four factors: perceived ability at a particular task is a function of the amount of success in the past at similar tasks, as would be predicted from Kelley's (1967) statement on attribution theory. According to Weiner *et al.*, task difficulty is inferred from the performance of others at the task; if many people succeed it will be perceived as easy, whereas if many fail it will be seen as difficult. If performance is consistent with these norms then behaviour is attributed to task difficulty, but an outcome which differs from the norm (e.g. succeeding at a task at which most people fail) will be attributed to personal characteristics and give rise to evaluative judgments. Luck is inferred from a variable pattern of past outcomes, whereas the perception of effort is more variable in that it may be dependent upon cues such as persistence in the task, muscular tension or even the outcome of the task: success leading to an attribution of high effort, and failure leading to an attribution of lack of effort.

In addition to discussing these attribution conditions and supporting them with experimental evidence (e.g. Feather, 1961; Bennion, 1961; Jones, Rock, Shaver, Goethals and Ward, 1968; Weiner and Kukla, 1970), Weiner *et al.* introduce achievement motivation as a personality variable into their attributional model. Those high in achievement motivation are said to be attracted to achievement-related activities which allow the attribution of success to ability and effort – internal or dispositional attributions. These individuals persist in the face of failure, since this is seen as due to lack of effort, and they select tasks of intermediate difficulty since this allows the greatest self evaluative feedback. (Too difficult a task may lead to failure, but too easy a task gives no sense of accomplishment.) On the other hand, people who are low in achievement motivation are less attracted to achievement-related tasks, since success is more likely to be attributed to the external factors, task difficulty and luck; they give up when they fail due to a belief that failure comes through lack of ability; they select easy or difficult tasks, neither of which provide information on which to base self evaluation; and they tend not to try hard since they believe that success is unrelated to effort.

(b) *Clinical psychology and attribution of success and failure*

A fairly obvious extension into applied psychology has been made in the form of some of the work described above. This aspect of attribution theory is unusual in that it has centred around personality variables, and again this allows it to be extended to clinical psychology. Important variables relevant here are the locus of control dimension (Rotter, 1966) and learned helplessness (Seligman, 1972, 1975).

Many studies have investigated relationships between behaviour pathologies and locus of control. External subjects – those who attribute the rewards they receive to external events (luck or fate, for example) – are less realistic than internal subjects in their handling of success and failure, and are less capable of coping with their environment (Phares, 1976). Presumably, a subject who does not attribute any reinforcements he may receive to his own behaviour is less likely to adjust his behaviour to the particular environment he is in. He may also be less able to learn from successes and failures if he attributes them to external causes. In addition, several studies (e.g. Butterfield, 1964; Feather, 1967; Watson, 1967; Strassberg, 1973), have concluded that externality has a high correlation with anxiety, perhaps because external subjects do not attribute their successes and failures to themselves and may therefore have a high expectancy of punishment (Phares, 1976).

An additional clinical concept, that of 'learned helplessness' (Seligman, 1972, 1975), has been linked to the attribution of success and failure. This concept represents an inability to respond effectively, reflecting a learned expectancy that any response will be ineffective. Seligman maintains that clinical depression may be explained in this way, and if this is so, changing the type of attributions of success and failure made by depressive patients could be a method of treatment. This view is supported in a study by Klein, Fencil-Morse, and Seligman (1976) who showed that subjects could be induced to behave in a similar fashion to depressives, having first undergone learning experiences similar to those assumed to underlie the development of depression. Depressed and non-depressed students took part in the study by performing a discrimination task consisting of either four soluble or four insoluble problems. A control group received no problems. Among subjects who received insoluble problems, some were given instructions to attribute their failure internally, ('most people are able to get three or four of the problems correct'), some were given instructions to attribute failure externally ('the problems are very difficult and almost no one has been able to solve them'), while some received no attributional instructions. In a second phase of the experiment all subjects were given an anagram task. As might be expected, non-depressed performed better than depressed subjects, and those who previously received soluble problems performed better than those who had received insoluble problems. Non-depressed subjects who had received insoluble problems performed similarly in the anagram task to depressives who had been in the soluble problem or control groups. The attribution instructions had little effect on non—depressed subjects, but depressives who were able to attribute their failure externally performed better than those given internal attribution instructions, or those given no instructions. It appears, therefore, from this study, that helplessness can indeed be learned, and that it can be alleviated by attributing failure externally.

(c) *Attribution of success and failure related to educational problems*

It is readily apparent that the way educational successes and failures are attributed both by the student and the teacher will markedly affect future educational behaviour. Some of the work in attribution theory that has already been reviewed supports this case. For example, Weiner *et al.* (1971) have maintained that high achievement orientated behaviour is related to internal attribution of success and failure, whereas low achievement orientated behaviour is related to external attribution of success, and the attribution of failure internally to lack of ability. The implications behind these proposals are that effective learning in an educational setting (high achievement orientated behaviour), will be more likely if the student attributes his successes and failures to himself: his successes to high ability and effort, and his failures to a modifiable lack of effort. Weiner *et al.* suggest that different attributional patterns which might lead to varying educational achievements may be differentially represented in social class or racial groups. In support of this suggestion, they quote Katz (1967) who describes low achieving negro boys as having been socialized to impose failure upon themselves. Thus, if it is the case that attributional processes have an important role in educational achievement, as seems likely, then not only can they help to understand and predict that achievement, but they might be involved in some kind of remedial programme for a failing student.

As regards description of a student's abilities and achievements made by teachers, a number of studies indicate that such attributions can have an important effect on later educational achievements, such that the attributions may become self-fulfilling prophecies. For example, the well-known study by Rosenthal and Jacobson (1968) showed that when various pupils were randomly designated as 'spurters', then this favourable expectation on the part of teachers caused dramatic gains in IQ. While Snow (1969) has pointed out a number of methodological and statistical flaws in the Rosenthal and Jacobson study, subsequent research (e.g. Meichenbaum, Bowers and Ross, 1969; Rubovits and Maehr, 1971, 1973), has indicated an important and startling effect of teachers' attributions on students' later achievements. Meichenbaum *et al.* suggest that the effect may be mediated by the positive and encouraging quality of the teacher–pupil interaction; in a rather different light, but by no means contradictory to this, Weiner *et al.* use their own attributional model to offer an explanation in terms of the teacher believing that occasional failures by the assumedly highly able pupils were due to lack of effort, rather than lack of ability. Such a pattern of attributions characterized individuals with high achievement motivation which may in fact be introjected by the pupils and facilitate achievement orientated behaviour.

The study of the attribution of success and failure has lent itself admirably to applied psychology, particularly clinical and educational problems. In many respects this is due to the apparent relation of certain personality variables to the way failures and successes are ascribed. It is clear that this is an important aspect of attribution theory, if only because of its extension into the applied field. Nevertheless, there are considerations which lead one to question whether clinical and educational psychologists should allow themselves to be influenced unduly by this work. These considerations revolve around the question of whether attributions are accurate, and will be discussed in the next section and in the conclusion to the chapter.

5 Primacy effects in attribution

Some of the studies reviewed in the last section are startling and worrying because the large effects they demonstrate are produced by such minimal information. For example, Rosenthal and Jacobson were able to show large gains in IQ in selected pupils, merely by telling teachers that these particular pupils were likely to be 'spurters'. If, as seems to be the case, this effect is mediated by the quality of subsequent teacher–pupil interaction, it is all the more remarkable that the initial attribution (i.e. 'a spurter') was not modified or restrained by that subsequent interaction.

This so-called 'primacy' effect, causing an initial attribution to prevent others which might be based on more information, appears to be fairly widespread (Jones and Goethals, 1971), and is particularly effective in influencing judgments of ability, or other characteristics which are expected to be relatively stable and consistent over time.

Jones and Goethals describe three processes which may account for the primacy effect: attention decrement, discounting and assimilation. The first, attention decrement, may occur as a kind of selective attention allowing a person who observes another's behaviour actively to ignore behaviour that is incompatible with an earlier attribution.

Attention decrement is said to be most likely under cognitive overload: when a person needs to simplify all available information. Discounting later information appears to depend on that information being inconsistent with an attribution already made. Assimilation is a more active process, which Jones and Goethals liken to assimilation in more general cognitive psychology by assuming 'that information creates, or finds its way into pre-existing, categories....Once a categorical decision is made, subsequent evidence is distorted to fit the category ... as long as it is not too discrepant from the category's typical instance' (p.43). All three processes, it can be seen, are mechanisms to ensure consistent attributions.

The primacy effect can be explained in terms of cognitive overload, as Jones and Goethals implied in relation to attention decrement; a person has too much to remember and needs to simplify available information. It may be more economical in terms of 'cognitive effort' to use pre-existing categories and to distort evidence to fit them rather than to use new contradictory information which requires different categories to be adopted. Thus it is likely that once a person is described as 'intelligent' his later behaviour will be assimilated to this category. Kanouse (1971) has pointed out that it is very unusual to change attributions, so if this person's later behaviour cannot be ascribed to his being intelligent then it may be attributed to situational conditions. A final explanation of the primacy effect comes from Kanouse who suggests that we may have a tendency to assume a single cause for behaviour. Once a cause has apparently been found in the initial attribution, there can be little reason to look for another cause.

6 Conclusion: consistency in attributions

In the last fifteen years, social psychology has been dominated by the development of attribution theory. This chapter has dealt with some aspects of this now large area, and it merely remains, in conclusion, to discuss how these aspects are related in their common function of tending towards consistent evaluations of the person whose behaviour is being observed.

As outlined at the beginning of this chapter, Allport's (1937) attention to the large number of trait words which can be used in our language to describe personality characteristics has shown the importance of attributions of behaviour. A simple description of behaviour could scarcely require such a repertoire: there must be a more important function than mere description when such an immense choice of trait words is available.

As mentioned previously in this chapter, the important functions of attributions are to evaluate past behaviour, and predict future behaviour. Heider (1958) proposed that man attempts to see his social environment as predictable and controllable, and that the latter is a result of predictability; attributions, then, allow him to make sense of the world. Heider is by no means the only psychologist to emphasize this aspect of behaviour. Kelly (1955) has claimed that man is a scientist, aiming to predict and control events by forming hypotheses, and testing them against his perceptions of reality. These hypotheses, or constructs, appear to be analogous, at least in function, to attributions in that they allow not only a description of behaviour or other events, but also its evaluation and prediction. To give some indication of their importance, the fundamental postulate of Kelly's theory claims that man tries to make sense of the world so that he can predict and control events. Kelly's work implies that man's cognitive behaviour is primarily, and perhaps entirely, directed towards this end. Hence the importance of attributions.

The vital function of attributions thus includes a number of aspects, yet they are remarkably brief. When, for example, it is said that, 'Mrs S. is dim-witted', it is reported that Mrs S. has emitted some behaviour which does not seem to be the result of much intelligent thought, that the behaviour is not greatly admired although it can probably be tolerated, and that similar behaviour is expected in future. The original attribution is an excellent shorthand for all that it implies. Thus the use of personality traits and characteristics in our language is a code or simplification of description, evaluation, and prediction of behaviour. One may suspect that such simplification is necessary because of the widespread and important use of attributions, and their various functions.

There are in fact a number of aspects of the attribution process which lead to the conclusion that it is essentially one of simplification. First, trait words are used as a kind of code for all that an attribution implies, as already discussed. Second, there is an important tendency, the primacy effect, for attributions, once made, to be maintained. As mentioned in an earlier section, Jones and Goethals propose that this tendency, in which ever way it is upheld, has the function of simplifying the information which a person must remember, and of reducing inconsistency.

Thus it is argued that the process of attribution is one which tends toward consistency. In the first instance, as already discussed, attributions though based on observation and description are really inferences about behaviour. Inference implies some judgmental process, and, as seen in the previous chapter, social judgments have a tendency to be consistent. Secondly, it has been shown that attributions are a form of shorthand which is used to reduce cognitive overload. In a different area of social psychology, that of balance theory, it has been shown (e.g. Cottrell, 1975; Picek, Sherman and Shiffrin, 1975; Sherman and Wolosin, 1973), that consistent information reduces cognitive overload. Applied to attribution theory, this would lead us to expect that attributions are most likely to be evaluatively and descriptively consistent. Just such a conclusion has been reached by various workers (e.g. Felipe, 1970; Peabody, 1970) who argue that both evaluative and descriptive consistency have important independent influences on the way traits are ascribed. Felipe proposed that traits which are descriptively similar, or consistent (e.g. extravagant and generous) are more likely to be thought of as occurring together in a person, irrespective of their evaluations, than traits which are evaluatively consistent but descriptively inconsistent (e.g. thrifty and generous). Further to this, traits which are both descriptively and evaluatively consistent are more likely to be seen as occurring together than are those which are only descriptively but not evaluatively consistent.

Much of the work relating to attribution theory has

investigated the conditions under which personal as opposed to situational attributions are made. All of the major statements (e.g. Heider, 1958; Jones and Davis, 1965; Kelley, 1967), emphasize this distinction, although it is also clear that personal attributions are favoured (Heider, 1958). It therefore appears that, as laymen, we have a tendency to attribute behaviour to the person rather than the situation he is in, provided that the person is not ourself (Jones and Nisbett, 1971). According to Mischel (1968) psychologists have the same tendency, and it may be instructive to investigate its function.

Jones and Davis suggest that personal attributions allow the most correspondent (or consistent) inferences between behaviour, intentions and personality. They are therefore preferred presumably because consistent attributions allow future behaviour to be predicted most easily, although this does not imply most accurately. It is tempting to assume that personal attributions made by psychologists, as professionals, may have a similar function. Mischel claims that personality theorists rarely consider the effect of the situation when outlining the causes of behaviour, but place most emphasis on a personal approach. This accusation implies that what the professional psychologist is doing is making personal attributions, for example, 'neurotic, introvert' (Eysenck, 1961) which imply consistent behaviour whose description and evaluation can be simplified to trait words. It is perhaps worth remembering that it is actually the job of many psychologists to describe and evaluate a patient's or client's past behaviour – but above all to predict his future behaviour. The most 'natural' way to do this would be to use the layman's method of making personal attributions, which are conveniently consistent, provide least cognitive load, and give the assumption that the behaviour is explained and predictable.

Social psychology is unable to give an answer to the question of whether attributions are accurate, because it is difficult to be objective about whether a person is or is not, for example, 'highly strung'. One cannot therefore condemn professional psychologists who make personal attributions as inaccurate, at least on the basis of attribution theory. However it should be remembered that it is the patient who is labelled, for example, 'extrovert', rather than the particular behaviour that the psychologist was, in reality, describing, and that this label can be applied to the patient for a long time: psychologists, like laymen, have a primacy effect in their attributions. Szasz (1972) has argued that labelling has had a distressing effect on the treatment of mental illness. Further, it is notable that views such as those of Laing (1959), that psychiatric disorders are caused by insane *situations,* have had comparatively little support from clinical psychology. However, it is not the intention, here, to give a full discussion of the controversy between the so-called 'trait-state' as opposed to the situationalist (Mischel, 1968) views of personality; (for such a discussion see, for example, Argyle and Little, 1972; Bowers, 1973; Hampson, 1982; Mischel, 1973). It is merely intended to point out that the layman's preference for personal attributions, which allow a consistent description, explanation and prediction of behaviour, appears to be copied strikingly well by professional psychologists with apparently similar results.

The function of attributions, therefore, is not mere description, but evaluation and prediction of behaviour. Most commonly, these functions are performed by single personality trait words which allow immense simplification of all they imply. The prevalence of personal attributions by laymen and psychologists alike allows consistent attributions to be made, which in turn imply that behaviour is seen as, and expected to be, stable and predictable.

4 Interpersonal attraction

I Introduction

It is apparent that among the most important aspects of our world are other people: they provide us with friendship, love, happiness and other positive experiences, and also with negative experiences such as disliking, hate, pain and unhappiness. It is therefore to be expected that we will have learned to make judgments about those people with whom we come into contact. Frequently these judgments will include a descriptive element as well as an evaluation; such judgments are called, by social psychologists, 'attributions', and have been considered in Chapter 3; this chapter will consider another type of judgment, the kind which is often described in terms of liking or friendship and their opposites. Psychological studies of interpersonal attraction have mainly concerned bonds between people based upon liking or friendship (how they are formed, for example, or what factors influence them). Some workers have included within this topic studies of romantic love, but since the theoretical explanations which are applicable to liking and friendship can seldom be applied to romantic love (see, for example, Berscheid and Walster, 1974; Rubin, 1970, 1973), this aspect of attraction will not be considered in this chapter, except for brief mentions in instances where it has influenced studies of friendship formation.

Theories of attraction can be divided into those that stem from the principle of consistency (e.g. Heider, 1958; Newcomb, 1953), and those that invoke explanations in terms of behaviourism and reinforcement principles (e.g. Byrne, 1961a; Thibaut and Kelley, 1959). This chapter discusses these two types of theory in turn; it also deals with the factors influencing attraction as they appear most relevant to the theories, and concludes with a comparative evaluation of the two approaches to the explanation of interpersonal attraction.

2 Dyadic balance

Heider's (1944, 1958) balance theory is the earliest and simplest of the consistency theories. Its main concern, judging by subsequent research, has been attitude organization, which Heider dealt with in terms of triadic balance. The philosophical bases of balance theory and the way it relates to attitudes have been considered in detail in Chapter 2. However, Heider was equally concerned with dyadic balance, which he described as characterizing a situation in which two people either both liked each other, or both disliked each other. Balanced situations were thought to be pleasant, tension-free, and not inducing pressure towards changing one of the liking or disliking relationships. A dyad in which the relationships between the two people, P and O, were different (for example, P liked O but O disliked P) Heider would consider unbalanced, and as such should be unpleasant, tension provoking and easily changed.

Heider's theory is an example of a social-psychological theory which perhaps states the obvious: it *is* pleasant when two people both like each other, and it *is* unpleasant when liking is not reciprocated. The theory deals with cognitions rather than actual events; that is, Heider is saying that balance is a function of how we *think* relationships are, and that we think unbalanced situations are unpleasant. It is scarcely surprising therefore that the theory appears a little obvious, since if it did not Heider would have totally misjudged our cognitions. However, the transparency of the theory makes it neither irrelevant nor useless, as there are a number of interesting questions which one may formulate within its framework.

For example, one may question whether dyadic balance is a concept that is appropriate to cognitions only, or whether it is applicable to real life as well; and also whether the situation can be influenced by factors other than balance, for instance, perhaps it is preferable to be liked even if the other person is not very likeable himself. In addition, research dealing with dyadic balance has thrown some light on negative relationships indicating that 'disliking' may in fact be more neutral than might originally be supposed (Price, Harburg and Newcomb, 1966). Studies which deal with these points will now be reviewed.

In Blumberg's (1969) study, for example, subjects were asked to rate various situations for pleasantness. These situations described different people whom the subjects had identified by their initials as their best friend, a friend moderately liked, a person slightly liked, and a disliked person. These four levels of liking were paired with four levels of the subject being liked by the identified person and each situation was rated for pleasantness. Blumberg termed a situation, or dyad, asymmetrical if the levels of liking of the two relations were not identical. His data indicated that subjects considered that it was more pleasant to be in a symmetrical dyad, thus supporting balance theory. Situations in which subjects liked the other person, but were particularly well liked in return were also, however, rated as pleasant; and this does not agree with balance theory. We do not, however, find it particularly surprising. An explanation might be given in terms of 'being liked' being a socially approved characteristic. This situation therefore agrees with the subjects' assumptions as to what is appropriate, and it is therefore pleasant. This may be an example of how prevailing norms may influence, even override, particular biases such as balance, and thereby influence individuals' perceptions of relationships. A similar explanation may account for the highly significant 'positivity effect' in Blumberg's results; he found not only that people preferred to be liked, but also that they preferred to like others. This positivity effect has been found in many studies which have investigated balance theory (e.g. Gutman and Knox, 1972; Jordan, 1953; Whitney, 1971; Zajonc and Burnstein, 1965), and demonstrates a not very surprising finding: liking is a pleasant relationship.

A further study which considered balance in dyads is that of Miller and Geller (1972). This differed from Blumberg's experiment in that the relations between two fictitious people were described to subjects, who were then asked to predict how these relations would be at some future time. The subjects were also asked to rate the degree of tension that they perceived in the dyad. The relations used also differed from those in Blumberg's experiment, since they were given as liking, disliking, ambivalence and neutrality. Subjects expected that the relations between the hypothetical people would be more stable when they were mutual, and the stability data therefore supported balance theory. The tension data, however, were less conclusive. Although the dyad which was balanced by containing two liking relations was seen as the least tense, the most tense was not an unbalanced dyad, but one in which both relations were disliking. These data are therefore less supportive of balance theory than are Blumberg's.

A further approach to the investigation of dyadic balance was made in a study by Price, Harburg and Newcomb (1966). In addition to their main study (which concerned triadic balance) they asked subjects to identify (by initials) an individual whom they would call their best friend, and an individual whom they disliked. Dyadic balance was tested by asking the subjects to say whether they thought that these individuals liked or disliked them in return. Ninety-eight per cent of the subjects said that their best friend liked them, while 2 per cent did not know. No subject reported that his best friend disliked him. These data are therefore supportive of balance. A somewhat different result was obtained, however, when subjects were asked how the disliked person felt about them: 27 per cent thought that the dislike was returned, 26 per cent thought they were liked by the person whom they disliked, while 47 per cent did not know. Thus only about a quarter of the subjects produced responses which supported balance theory, and a similar number actually perceived existing dyads of which they were a member to be unbalanced.

These findings, while not readily interpreted by balance

theory, do provide support for the view that 'positivity bias' is important: people prefer to like others and to be liked by them. Such an interpretation is so obvious from everyday observation that it is difficult to find an explanation for it, and indeed social psychologists have failed to propose any explanations for the positivity bias. However, being in a positive relation may be more rewarding, or it may be a socially approved characteristic.

A phenomenon related to the positivity bias is that reported by Price, Harburg and Newcomb (1966), whose data suggest that subjects find it difficult to identify a disliked person. They propose that there is in fact ambivalence toward people whom subjects say they dislike: that is, when measured on a scale of liking, negative relations are rarely as extreme as positive relations.

The concept of the positivity bias, and the fact that people do not often dislike others, perhaps provide at least some of the reasons why dyadic balance is not always found. When positive reciprocated relations are reported, it must be remembered that balance and positivity are both evidenced, and therefore an adequate test of dyadic balance can only be carried out when a negative (or disliking) relationship is part of the dyad. Since this may be interpreted as ambivalent (e.g. Price, Harburg and Newcomb, 1966), any attempt at verifying dyadic balance may be ambiguous. Perhaps this is the most that can be concluded from experiments purporting to test dyadic balance.

3 Newcomb's (1953) theory of interpersonal communication

An early attempt to develop an explanation of attraction along consistency principles was that of Newcomb (1953). In many respects his theory has similarities to Heider's (1946, 1958) balance theory, which is considered in Chapter 2, but it is based on different principles, and clearly states that social interaction and attraction are best studied in relation to communication.

Newcomb's theory concerns two people in communication about a third entity X, which may be personal or non-personal. The relationship between the two people (A and B) cannot exist in an environmental vacuum, in that when A and B communicate they must be communicating about something (X). Newcomb asserts that relationships without communication cannot exist. In addition, a person who holds certain attitudes towards X must communicate about them in order to show them, and it is, according to Newcomb, a necessary condition of being human that attitudes are not held in a social vacuum.

This theory proposes, therefore, that there is a basic human tendency to communicate with others about one's attitudes, and that such communication is the basis of relationships with others. Newcomb's system, often called the 'ABX system', concerns both relationships in reality and cognitions about relationships, as compared to Heider's, which only deals with cognitions (see Chapter 2). Newcomb suggests that four relationships within the system must be considered: AB (that is, A's relationship to B), AX, BA and BX, and that these may be positive or negative (liking or disliking). The ABX system is characterized by an equilibrium of its relationships, such that a change in any one of them can lead to changes in others. Newcomb thus postulates that there are 'strains' (p.395) towards preferred states of equilibrium, just as Heider postulates a tendency towards balance. The greater the attraction between A and B – or, in other words, the greater liking – the greater is the strain towards symmetry. This is a state in which A and B have similar (either both liking or both disliking) relationships towards X, and such relationships are said to be 'symmetrical'. The theory suggests that there will be little strain towards symmetry unless there is a positive relation between A and B, which Newcomb terms 'attraction'. Further, when attraction between A and B is small the strain towards symmetry is limited to particular attitudinal objects (i.e. Xs) to which attitudinal relations are required by the association of A and B.

Newcomb suggests that the different systems which may be formed by variations in the four relationships he considers in the ABX system can be classified as 'symmetrical' (consistent); or 'in strain' (inconsistent). Symmetrical systems are those in which the relationships between A and B (AB and

BA) are positive and the attitudinal relations (AX and BX) are either both positive or both negative. Systems which are in strain are those in which there is a negative relation between A and B, or those in which there is one positive and one negative attitudinal relation.

As already pointed out, Newcomb (1953) views symmetrical ABX systems as produced through communication, and in later papers (Newcomb, 1956, 1959), he places even greater emphasis upon this. He suggests that interpersonal attraction can be predicted by a knowledge of particular variables such as frequency of interaction, attitudinal agreement, and perception of reciprocated interaction. The link between these variables and interpersonal attraction is that they are all related to the frequency of communication, and it is this, therefore, that determines interpersonal attraction.

A number of studies have reported evidence which supports Newcomb's theory. For example, it can be predicted that when a new group forms from people who are initially strangers, the members of this group will interact (thus becoming aware of each other's attitudes) and this communication should cause attraction to develop between those who have similar attitudes. Newcomb (1956) tested this with male college students who shared a house, by assessing their attitudes and liking of each other at various times during a sixteen-week period. Subjects' attitudes on a number of topics were investigated, and it appeared that pre-acquaintance similarities in attitude led to attraction between individuals towards the end of the sixteen weeks. The reverse relation (attraction leading to similar attitudes) was not found: there was little attitudinal change during the sixteen-week period. In a somewhat similar study, Newcomb (1943) had demonstrated that female students adopted the attitudes of those with whom they interacted in a small private college.

It is characteristic of Newcomb's investigations that real-life groups are studied as they become acquainted with each other on a relatively long-term basis. Such studies are obviously more time consuming and difficult to perform than the less life-like laboratory studies often used to support Heider's theory (for examples see Chapter 2). It is perhaps this aspect of Newcomb's work which allows one to have confidence in his theory, in spite of the relatively few studies which have attempted to support it.

However, although the number of studies which have been specifically designed to test Newcomb's theory is small, many others support the view that there exists a relation between attraction and communication. For example, strength of friendship can be predicted from a knowledge of amount of interaction (Gullahorn, 1952) and anticipated amount of interaction (Darley and Berscheid, 1967). In addition, Lott and Lott (1961) showed that friends are more likely to talk to each other in group discussions than are those who are not friends. None of these findings is particularly surprising, but together they suggest that the relationship between attraction and communication which Newcomb proposed does exist.

A group of studies that bear a certain similarity to Newcomb's work has been carried out by Duck (e.g. 1973, 1977; Duck and Spencer, 1972). This work is concerned with the way personality similarity relates to friendship formation, and it suggests that equivalence of personal constructs (Kelly, 1955) aids attraction. In a longitudinal study Duck and Craig (1978) tested the hypothesis that newly acquainted friends will be similar in terms of superficial personality characteristics, whereas long-term friendships are more likely to be explained by similarity of more fundamental personality characteristics. Student subjects living in a college residence were tested three times during the period of the study: first, after one month from the time of initial acquaintance; second, after three months; and finally, at the end of the study after eight months. At each testing occasion, subjects were asked for their sociometric choices amongst others in the subject pool, so as to ascertain friendships, and were given three personality tests: the California Psychological Inventory, the Allport-Vernon Study of Values and the Role Construct Repertory Grid Test. At the initial testing, after one month of acquaintance, none of the measures predicted sociometric choices. After three months friends were similar to each other on the scale of values but not on other measures. After eight months friends were similar on types of constructs used, but there were no significant effects on the other measures. Duck and Craig emphasize that their data indicate that no one measure of personality will explain attraction. What is required is the relative importance of each measure as a friendship develops. It appears that the basis for liking another person changes with the time of acquaintance. Again, it seems that studies such as that of Duck and Craig, and those of Newcomb, being longitudinal, are more informative than many short-term experiments about attraction.

4 Reactions to personal evaluations

As has been pointed out earlier in this chapter, we are continually making judgments and evaluations about other people, both as a way of interpreting their past and present behaviour and as a way of predicting their future behaviour (see Chapter 3). However, such judgments are not one-way: other people will necessarily be making evaluations of ourselves, and it is our reaction to these evaluations, and the way our liking of the evaluator is influenced, with which this section is concerned.

If a person makes some judgment about us, whether it be a general statement about our personality (e.g. 'What a horrid person you are'), or a more specific evaluation of particular behaviour (e.g. 'that was a very generous thing to do'), it is very likely to influence our liking or disliking of the person. One of the specific questions that social psychologists have asked in this area is whether we prefer evaluations of ourselves to be positive or favourable, regardless of whether we agree with the evaluator's opinion, or whether we prefer evaluations to support our own views of ourselves whether positive or negative.

The latter view would support a consistency framework and was in fact proposed by Secord and Backman (1965) as 'social congruity theory'. This theory suggests that we should be attracted to a person who is favourable towards something (in this case ourselves) of which we approve, or who is unfavourable towards something (again ourselves) of which we disapprove. As such it is a direct extension of Heider's (1958) balance theory in which the place of X in the POX triad (see Chapter 2) is taken by the self. From this one may deduce that a person who thinks favourably of himself (or has high self esteem) will like others who also evaluate him favourably. On the other hand a person who has an unfavourable opinion of himself (or has low self esteem) will like others who give him an unfavourable evaluation.

An experiment by Deutsch and Solomon (1959) is most often cited to support this position. Their subjects were led to believe that they had done well or poorly at a task which they had performed individually. This manipulation was designed to induce high or low self esteem. They were then given an evaluation of their performance supposedly made by another subject, but in fact designed to be very favourable or, alternatively, very unfavourable. Subjects' own evaluations of this other subject were the dependent variable, and indicated that those in whom high self esteem had been induced preferred others who evaluated their performance positively, whereas those in whom low self esteem had been induced preferred others with an unfavourable opinion of their performance.

Although this appears to be clear evidence for the social congruity theory, a later study (Skolnick, 1971) produced rather different results. With a very similar procedure, Skolnick demonstrated a tendency he termed 'signification', implying that people seek positive evaluations from others regardless of their own levels of self esteem. In Skolnick's results there was a slight tendency in the direction opposite to that predicted by social congruity theory, such that those in whom low self esteem had been induced had the strongest preference for positivity. Skolnick suggested that the difference between his experiment and that of Deutsch and Solomon lay in the degree of ego involvement and suspicion of the subjects. He proposed that balance theory will operate, as in the Deutsch and Solomon study, when there is low ego involvement in the task, and high suspicion. On the other hand, signification will occur when there is little suspicion and high ego involvement. In addition, Skolnick suggested that his subjects, who were students, might be more easily influenced by the manipulation of self esteem, which for them would be constantly changing, than would the subjects of the Deutsch and Solomon study, who were telephone operators, and might have a more stable self concept.

A further study using similar methodology (Dutton, 1972) failed to support Skolnick's signification hypotheses, but obtained evidence for social congruity theory when the task was unimportant. Subjects performing an important task showed consistency, but only when they had formed a stable evaluation of their own abilities, so that their self esteem was resistant to potential short-term changes made by experimental manipulations.

An experiment by Stroebe, Eagly and Stroebe (1977) also supported social congruity theory by demonstrating that inconsistency could be resolved by attributing it to experimental instructions. Subjects completed a personality test which allowed them to be classified as having high or low self esteem, and were then told that their responses were being shown to another subject who was going to give his impressions of them. This 'other subject' had been told either that he was to give his sincere impressions or that he was to write a character description of the subject which would be convincingly either positive or negative. All subjects were in fact given one of two notes describing either a favourable or an unfavourable character, and were then asked to say how likely it was that the 'other subject' had produced the description under role playing rather than sincere instructions. It appeared that all subjects thought the note less likely to be sincere if it did not agree with their own self evaluations. Thus high self esteem subjects thought a description less likely to be sincere if negative, whereas low self esteem subjects thought it less likely to be sincere if positive.

It appears that the majority of studies, with the exception of that of Skolnick (1971), have supported social congruity theory, indicating, perhaps, that subjects prefer consistency, so that their own self evaluations are confirmed. Unfortunately, the conclusion cannot be so straightforward. Firstly, as Skolnick has pointed out, there may be different experimental conditions which favour consistency as opposed to signification, and these may not become apparent until after data have been collected. Secondly, the manipulation of self esteem in the experiments reported often leaves much to be desired, and is seldom equivalent from one experiment to another. For example, the Deutsch and Solomon (1959) method of telling subjects that they had done well or poorly at a task may or may not induce high or low self esteem in the subject, presumably depending upon whether the subject himself interprets the task and the evaluation to be important. Even though similar methods have been used in later experiments (e.g. Skolnick, 1971) whether an equivalent effect is produced must depend on subjects' interpretations. A further problem is introduced when standardized tests of self esteem are used (e.g. Stroebe *et al.*, 1977) since Wells and Marwell (1976) report that these measures are seldom equivalent.

An additional complication arises if one considers a study by Hewitt and Goldman (1974). They showed that low self esteem subjects gave increased liking of another when evaluated positively by him, and decreased liking when evaluated negatively, as Skolnick would predict. However, the situation is more complex for subjects with high self esteem. These subjects could be differentiated into those with high and those with low Crowne and Marlowe (1960) social desirability scores. A high scorer on this scale is one who attempts to present himself in a favourable, rather than necessarily in an honest, way. It is just such a characteristic, Hewitt and Goldman suggest, which would allow some subjects to obtain high self esteem scores, since measures of self esteem often ask subjects if they are self-confident and competent in social relations. Thus subjects with high self esteem on such measures, and high Crowne and Marlowe scores, might well have low self esteem if measured accurately. Hewitt and Goldman in fact showed that such subjects behaved like their low self esteem subjects on another evaluation task. Subjects with 'accurate high self esteem' (those with measured high self esteem and low Crowne and Marlowe scores) did not change their liking for the other who evaluated them positively or negatively.

It seems from this confused picture that the most that can be concluded is that consistency is probably the major tendency in evaluating others who have given evaluations of ourselves, with the proviso that experimental conditions can be altered so as to make signification more important. In addition, the self esteem of the subject has been treated as an important variable, but one cannot claim that its measurement and manipulation have been controlled.

5 Physical attractiveness

One of the variables that has been investigated with respect to interpersonal attraction is physical attractiveness. There are, of course, many stereotypes about behavioural characteristics which are thought to be the result of physical characters; for example fat men are traditionally jolly, people with thin lips are thought not to be talkative (Secord and Muthard, 1955), and Shakespeare would have us believe that 'beauty lives with kindness' (*The Two Gentlemen of Verona,* IV, ii). Considering the pervasiveness of such beliefs it would be surprising if liking, being an important behavioural relationship, were unaffected by physical attraction.

It is obviously an oversimplification to speak of physical attractiveness as though it were a single variable, as many physical attributes must be involved in an overall impression of attractiveness. However, it is comparatively easy for subjects to make overall judgments of attractiveness, so that one does not necessarily need to take account of individual physical attributes. An additional problem is that different cultures and subcultures may have different norms about what is considered to be physically attractive. However, with a reasonably homogeneous subject sample, this should not be a problem, and any findings should be generalizable to other subcultures, regardless of the specific norms about physical attractiveness on which the data were based.

Walster, Aronson, Abrahams and Rottman (1966) put forward a proposal known as the 'matching hypothesis' which suggested that people should like others who are of approximately equal physical attractiveness to themselves. The rationale behind this hypothesis is that physical attractiveness can be seen as a valuable asset in a 'dating partner' – the type of friendship with which most of these studies deal. However, this valuable asset is, potentially at least, mutual, and a person's choice of partner should depend, therefore, not only on the partner's physical attractiveness but on his estimate of his own worth in terms of this asset. The matching hypothesis was tested by Walster *et al.* by randomly pairing student subjects at a computer dance. Students filled in questionnaires which were supposedly fed into a computer which would then match them for compatibility. Unbeknown to the students, judges rated them in terms of physical attractiveness when they came to buy their tickets for the dance. Halfway through the dance questionnaires were administered individually to subjects asking how well the partner was liked and whether future interactions were desired, on the supposition that the questionnaires were to evaluate the computer selection process. The data showed that more attractive partners were liked more, but this appeared to be unaffected by the physical attractiveness of the other partner, thus providing no support for the matching hypothesis.

It was reasoned by Walster *et al.* that the failure to support the matching hypothesis might be due to the circumstances of the computer dance: there was little chance of rejection during the dance of one partner by the other so that subjects may have assumed that they could aspire to interactions with an extremely attractive partner regardless of their own attractiveness. In addition they may have assumed that the computer had matched them, not necessarily in terms of physical attractiveness, but on other characteristics.

A further test of the matching hypothesis by Walster and Walster (1969) again used a computer dance but subjects were able to meet their partners beforehand. Subjects were also asked to indicate their preferences for the attractiveness of their prospective partner. This experiment, which allowed for possible rejection by the partner, did provide support for the matching hypothesis. However, a number of other studies (e.g. Berscheid, Dion, Walster and Walster, 1971; Huston, 1973; Kiesler and Baral, 1970), have given more ambiguous results. Huston (1973), for example, attempted to remove fear of rejection by the partner in one condition of the experiment. In this condition, each subject was required to choose a partner who had already seen the subject's photograph and indicated that he would accept the subject. These subjects, who were sure of their being accepted, chose more attractive partners. In a different condition, when acceptance was not assured, subjects who rated themselves as more attractive believed that they had a greater chance of being accepted by their chosen partner than those who rated themselves as less attractive. This part of Huston's study therefore supported the matching hypothesis, but it did not when actual choice of a partner was concerned.

One might conclude that the matching hypothesis has had little support except under conditions which, to say the least, are very specific. The studies in which it has been investigated have used extremely unusual circumstances, perhaps of necessity, but one doubts whether the results are generalizable to more usual forms of initiation of friendships. It may be that physical attractiveness is only an important characteristic when interpersonal attraction is in its initial stages, but the work of Murstein (1971) indicates matching in terms of physical attractiveness between marriage partners. This being so, one cannot dismiss the matching hypothesis as being invalid, but can only suggest that its demonstration appears to depend on unusual conditions.

6 Propinquity

It is perhaps too obvious to discuss that one can only become attracted to another person if circumstances allow one to come in contact with him or her. However, although one would expect a fair amount of evidence suggesting that this is so, it is less obvious why closeness should lead to liking.

Considering the evidence first, it has been shown that students are likely to become acquainted if they are assigned to adjacent classroom seats (Byrne and Buehler, 1955), which cannot be a very surprising finding. It appears that friendships are formed on the basis of the functional distance (dependent on the likelihood of contact) between dwellings (Festinger, Schachter and Back, 1950; Whyte, 1956). In addition it is possible to manipulate the physical environment in order to increase liking relations; for example, Byrne (1961b) showed students formed more friendships if each student changed his seat every seven weeks than if they remained in the same seats throughout the term.

A number of explanations have been offered for the relationship between friendship and propinquity. In the light of earlier sections of this chapter, perhaps the most apparent is the theory of interpersonal communication proposed by Newcomb (1953). Propinquity increases the likelihood of communication and therefore knowledge about each other's similar attitudes. The theory predicts that this should lead to attraction.

A further explanation is provided by the work of Zajonc (1968) on 'mere exposure', which suggests that increasing exposure to a stimulus leads to increasing positive effect. Data demonstrating this effect have been collected using a variety of stimuli including nonsense words and Chinese characters (Zajonc, 1968), Turkish words (Zajonc and Rajecki, 1969) and photographs of strangers (Wilson and Nakajo, 1965). Mere exposure to another person, on repeated occasions, should lead to increasingly positive evaluations to him; in other words, to attraction.

Another possible explanation of the effects of propinquity on attraction results from exchange theory (Thibaut and Kelley, 1959) which will be considered in more detail in a later section of this chapter. However, in relation to propinquity, exchange theory suggests that people who are close to each other in terms of physical distance have a low cost for initiating interactions between each other. Interaction is thus more likely, and in turn will make it more probable that behaviour that is rewarding to both will be discovered. In addition, Thibaut and Kelley propose that continued interaction with others who are physically close costs less in terms of time and effort than with those more distant. It thus seems that friendly relations which are maintained with others at a distance must be particularly rewarding. One does not, for example, travel two hundred miles to pass the time of day with an acquaintance, but one might chat to him over the garden fence.

A number of possible explanations have been suggested for the relationship between interpersonal attraction and propinquity, all being reasonably plausible and with experimental support for the theoretical positions they propose. It does not seem to be possible to give evidence in favour of one and against another of the explanations, and it may well be that the different explanations are all correct and add to the relatively strong effect that closeness has on interpersonal attraction.

7 Consistency and interpersonal attraction: a summary

So far, this chapter has considered work dealing with interpersonal attraction which can broadly be contained within a consistency framework. The major theories of interpersonal attraction which propose this (Heider, 1958; Newcomb, 1953) have been reviewed, with the conclusion that Heider's dyadic balance may sometimes be difficult to demonstrate experimentally because of the problem that the negative relation (disliking) may be interpreted as ambivalence (Price, Harburg and Newcomb, 1966). Nevertheless, this is a problem for experimental demonstration rather than a direct criticism of consistency theory. Newcomb's theory, also firmly within the consistency framework, proposes a relationship between attraction and communication. Those few experiments (e.g. Newcomb, 1943, 1956) which have attempted to demonstrate the theory have been long-term and strongly supportive, such that one can place a great deal of confidence in Newcomb's ideas that it is a basic human tendency to communicate with others about our attitudes, and that this communication forms the backbone of our interpersonal relationships with those others.

Consistency also appears to be an important tendency when evaluating others who have given an evaluation of ourselves. However, a variety of conditions can affect this tendency such that positivity, or signification (Skolnick, 1971), becomes more important in that we like others who give us a positive evaluation on some characteristic, regardless of how we ourselves evaluate that characteristic. A more usual tendency, however, is that of consistency: we like others who agree with us about our characteristics, whether that agreement is in terms of positive or negative evaluations.

Subsequent sections of this chapter considered physical

attractiveness and propinquity. It seems that, at least in the initial stages of friendship, a physically attractive person is liked more than an unattractive one. The 'matching hypothesis' (Walster, Aronson, Abrahams and Rottman, 1966) suggested that we like others who are of approximately equal attractiveness to ourselves; this hypothesis has had little support except in some rather unusual conditions. To be fair to this hypothesis, it is difficult to see how it could be tested at all without the help of such conditions. Propinquity also appears to initiate and increase interpersonal attraction. Whatever explanation (or collection of explanations), is adopted to explain these relationships between liking and both propinquity and physical attractiveness, these relationships can well be interpreted within a consistency framework, in that the *Gestalt* notions of balance (Heider, 1958) include matching, similarity and closeness as characteristics of a good *Gestalt*, and therefore of a balanced or consistent situation. It therefore seems that the relationships between liking and propinquity and physical attractiveness are compatible and support the notion of consistency.

8 Byrne's (1961a) reinforcement theory of attraction

While the earlier parts of this chapter dealt with theories of interpersonal attraction which rely on consistency principles, the remaining sections of the chapter are concerned with theories which utilize the concept of reinforcement and behaviourist ideas.

At an initial glance, Byrne's (1961a) theory of attraction is remarkably similar to Newcomb's (1953) theory of interpersonal communication, in that Byrne proposes that attraction between people is a function of the similarity of their attitudes. However, it is important in this theory, not only that people are attracted to those with whom they agree, but that the basis of this attraction is reinforcement. That is, agreement with another person is rewarding because it allows a person to confirm his beliefs. This reward becomes associated with the other person, thus leading to liking: disagreement with another is punishing, which similarly becomes associated with the other person, leading to disliking.

Byrne's research programme which has been developed to support his reinforcement theory has followed a remarkably constant theme. In his first experiment (1961a) student subjects completed a scale which measured their attitudes on twenty-six different topics (e.g. belief in God, interest in sports, preference for political parties, classical music). They also indicated which they considered to be the thirteen most important and the thirteen least important topics. Following this, two weeks later, each subject was given a copy of the scale, supposedly completed by a stranger. In fact the scales they received were carefully designed so that in one group subjects received scales which were identical to those they had completed themselves, while for a second group the scales were opposite to those the subjects had completed. A third group received scales with answers the same as their own on topics they had considered important, but opposite on topics they had considered unimportant. A fourth group received scales with answers opposite to their own on important topics and the same on unimportant ones. Subjects then rated this 'stranger' on how much they thought they would like him, how much they would enjoy working with him, and how intelligent, knowledgeable, moral and well adjusted he was.

After combining the liking and enjoyment of working with the stranger into a single liking score, Byrne showed that the stranger with similar attitudes was liked better, and that he was rated as more intelligent, knowledgeable, moral and well-adjusted. The stranger agreeing only on important issues was seen as more moral and better adjusted, and slightly more likeable, than those agreeing only on unimportant issues.

There are various notable points concerning this first experiment in Byrne's research programme. First, the same general design and dependent variables were used in later experiments (e.g. Byrne, 1962; Byrne and Clore, 1966; Byrne and Nelson, 1965) so as to make them directly comparable. Second, the results do not actually tell one any more than could be predicted from Newcomb's (1953) theory of interpersonal communication; although Byrne's theory proposes that the basis of attraction is reinforcement (and this is its basic difference from Newcomb's theory), his study does not concern this important point of his theory. A final point is that in comparison to the long-term and more realistic studies undertaken by Newcomb (e.g. 1943, 1956), Byrne's research paradigm appears remarkably contrived, and one senses that he is perhaps only interested in the psychology of learning about strangers who are never actually met. (However, to be fair, it is by no means the only contrived research paradigm in social psychology.)

Later studies have stressed the reinforcement aspects of the theory. For example, Byrne and Clore (1967) suggested that agreement with others is rewarding because it implies that one's view of the world is confirmed and not threatened, and therefore supplies consensual validation. This was tested by having subjects in three different situations which attempted to vary the need an individual would have for consensual validation. In one condition subjects were confronted with attitude responses of a stranger which were different from their own; in a second condition their expectations regarding their performance on an intelligence test were disconfirmed; and in a third subjects viewed meaningless and confused films. Following the manipulation, the standard procedure was used for assessing attraction to strangers with varying attitude similarity, with the hypothesis that greater attraction should result from the greatest need for consensual validation. However, the results indicated that the condition which aroused the most need for consensual validation actually lessened the effect of similarity on attraction, whereas the greatest effect was found in the moderate condition.

A further experiment (Byrne, Young and Griffitt, 1966) attempted to demonstrate that attitude similarity is rewarding by using attitude statements as reinforcements in a discrimination learning task. However, Stalling (1970) disputed this result, showing that it is the positive or negative connotations of attitude statements, rather than their similarity or dissimilarity with the subject's beliefs, which are rewarding or punishing.

A further aspect of Byrne's work has been the effect of combining various rewards and punishments from a single person: in other words, what happens when another person holds some attitudes which are similar to one's own, and others which are different? Byrne and Nelson (1965) proposed and demonstrated that the degree of attraction towards the other person is directly related to the proportion of similar attitudes (rather than the actual number of similar attitudes) implying that attitudes on any issue are of equal importance for attraction – a point which everyday experience seems to defy. However, an additional study (Nelson, 1965) showed that the degree of disagreement is also a relevant variable in the determination of attraction. Later work has stated more formally the relation between attraction and positive and negative reinforcements as follows: 'attraction towards X is a positive linear function of the sum of the weighted positive reinforcements (Number X Magnitude) received from X divided by the total number of weighted positive and negative reinforcements received from X' (Byrne, 1969, p.76).

So far this discussion has considered similarity in terms of attitudes (as has Byrne's research); but other dimensions of similarity have also been used. These include questions about personal finances (Byrne, Griffitt and Stefaniak, 1967), socioeconomic levels, answers on the repression–sensitization scale (Byrne, 1964) and a self concept scale (Byrne, 1969).

In concluding this discussion on Byrne's reinforcement theory it seems that the main theme in the work following the initial statement of the theory has been the development of a formula to account for combinations of rewards and punishments and their relation to attraction, and the demonstration that similarity of attitudes (or other characteristics) is rewarding because it aids consensual validation of attitudes. The latter theme is the crux of the theory. As already discussed, there have been problems in attempting to demonstrate the reinforcing nature of similarity and dissimilarity (see also Eiser, 1980).

However damaging such problems may be, it is surely the experimental paradigm which is the downfall of this theory. Using a single paradigm for a series of experiments does, of course have its advantages – primarily that different studies are directly comparable. However, one of Byrne's early assumptions was that his theoretical constructs refer to experimental rather than real life variables. Any profits which may accrue as a result of this assumption are almost certainly outweighed by the disadvantages of abandoning an approximation to real life. The paradigm gives the impression of a closed experimental system such that there seems to be no resemblance between real life and the experiments. For example, subjects do not expect to meet the 'stranger', and their liking or disliking can therefore be only academic, in that it can have no consequence for a future relationship. Placed in such an extraordinary social vacuum, subjects can only speculate upon what is required of them, and since few responses are available, it is hardly surprising that Byrne obtains such regular results on so many occasions.

9 Social exchange theory

(a) *Basic concepts in the theory*

A more elaborate theory, relevant to interpersonal attraction, but also dealing with other aspects of social behaviour, has been proposed by Thibaut and Kelley (1959) and Homans (1961). This is social exchange theory. To be accurate, Thibaut and Kelley called their approach a 'framework' rather than a theory, implying that they are providing a method of looking at interpersonal relationships rather than a detailed theory. However, their proposals are vastly more detailed than Byrne's reinforcement theory, and cover more aspects of social behaviour, while remaining within the cover of behaviourism.

The general thesis of social exchange is that within dyads (or larger groups) interaction is part of a bargaining or trading relationship. A basic assumption is that a relationship is voluntarily entered into and prolonged only if it is satisfactory in terms of the costs paid to continue the relationship and the rewards gained from it. This economic terminology is no accident. Social exchange theory stresses that all human behaviour is a function of its pay-off, by being dependent on the amount and kind of reward and punishment which it produces.

In addition to using economic concepts, social exchange theory is firmly based within behaviourist psychology. Homans makes the assumption that social behaviour can be rewarded or punished by the behaviour of another person. For Thibaut and Kelley the similar assumption is that 'most socially significant behaviour will not be repeated unless it is reinforced, rewarded in some way' (1959, p.5).

Apart from rewards and costs, other concepts basic to exchange theory are outcomes, and comparison level. The outcome, or profit, of any particular behaviour or relationship is the rewards less the costs incurred as a result of the behaviour, or relationship. The comparison level (CL) is the standard against which relationships are judged. If the outcome of a particular relationship is more positive than a person's CL then he will be satisfied with that relationship and it is likely to result in interpersonal attraction. However, if the outcome is more negative than the CL then the relationship causes dissatisfaction. The CL is actually an average value of all the outcomes which a person has experienced, each outcome being weighted in terms of its salience for the individual person concerned. Included in the averaging process to obtain the CL are influences determined by past and present experiences with a variety of relationships as well as outcomes which the person judges other people to experience. The CL is therefore an idiosyncratic judgmental point, since individuals will vary in their experiences. In addition, Upshaw (1967) has shown that there are individual differences in the characteristic saliences of costs and rewards.

An additional concept which is used to determine the continuance of a relationship is the comparison level for alternatives (CLalt.). This is seen as the position of the outcome which a person believes he could experience in the most satisfying of any alternative relationships available to him. If the outcome of an existing relationship is below, or less satisfactory, than the person's CLalt., then it would be predicted that he would leave that relationship, in favour of the alternative more satisfying one. However, this does not necessarily imply that only satisfying relationships are continued, since the outcome of any particular relationship may be below the CL, and therefore unsatisfactory, but above the CLalt., and therefore the best relationship available.

Thibaut and Kelley (1959) suggest that one may study the interaction of a dyad by using a matrix to represent possible outcomes for each behaviour of each person. The outcomes typically depend on the behaviour of each member of the dyad, and can be represented numerically within the matrix. A typical matrix, in which members A and B of the dyad have a repertoire of two possible behaviours, is shown in Figure 4.1. The outcome for member A is given in the upper part of the cell, and the outcome for B is given in the lower part of the cell.

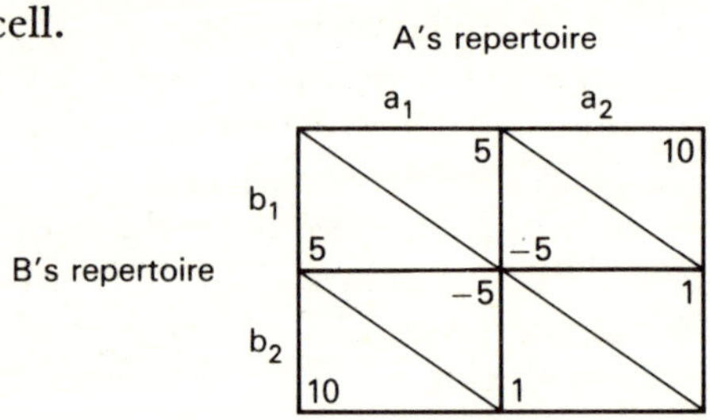

FIGURE 4.1 A matrix of outcomes of the possible interactions within a dyad, where each member may have one of two responses

The matrix shows that if A engages in behaviour a_1 and B in behaviour b_1, then both members receive an outcome of 5. However, if A engages in behaviour a_1, B can substantially increase his outcome to 10, and reduce A's outcome to -5 by emitting b_2. Similarly if B emits b_1, A may reply with a_2, so gaining a large outcome (10) for himself and a small outcome (-5) for B. Typically, this type of matrix which conforms to the rules of the Prisoner's Dilemma Game, causes the interaction which may be seen in terms of competition to 'lock' into the competitive a_2/b_2 cell of the matrix, both members ensuring that their partner will not gain an undue advantage over them (e.g. Deutsch and Krauss, 1960).

The power that each member of a dyad has over his partner (in terms of the member's interactions) can be represented by different numerical outcomes in the matrix. In addition, more complicated matrices can be portrayed showing larger behavioural repertoires of the participants, and, indeed, more than two participants. However, such complexities still rely on the basic social exchange approach: that satisfaction (and therefore interpersonal attraction) within a relationship depends on rewards and costs incurred, and judgmental standards used for comparison of the outcome.

(b) *Research relating interpersonal attraction to exchange theory*

Social exchange theory has been used widely in the explanation of interpersonal relationships, focusing on interactions between individuals, rather than characteristics of individuals. It is by no means confined to the study of attraction, and has been applied to social power, bargaining, conformity behaviour, status and esteem (e.g. Homans, 1961).

In specifically dealing with interpersonal attraction, Thibaut and Kelley outline four stages through which a relationship may pass. Initially, individuals explore potential costs and rewards available in relationships with others in a *sampling* stage. This sampling is likely to be among people who are physically close since (in exchange theory terms) the costs of relationships with such people are likely to be lower than with those who are at a greater distance. A study by Jennings (1943) concerning the relationships formed by delinquent girls showed that those who were chosen most by other girls for social relationships were those who sought out situations in which they were likely to meet others. This suggests that the more an individual samples others the more he is likely to form relationships with them.

The following stage, *bargaining*, takes place when interaction begins, and is in the form of giving and receiving rewards to discover whether it will be profitable to enter into a deeper relationship. Many aspects of interpersonal attraction considered earlier in this chapter are explicable in terms of the bargaining stage of relationships. For example, people with similar attitudes and values, or from similar backgrounds, are likely to be attracted to each other, as Byrne (1961a) would suggest, but this is interpreted by exchange theory as being due to the relatively high rewards and low costs associated with this type of relationship.

More long-term relationships involve a state of *commitment*. Sampling and bargaining with others is reduced, and a particular other is chosen for a certain type of relationship. Such relationships tend to be between equals, whether in terms of status (Homans, 1961) or popularity (Jennings, 1943). Kiesler (1966) has suggested that when two people interact continually, as would be the case in a committed relationship, they become able to predict each other's behaviour, and such predictability leads to attraction. This may be due to predictability lowering the costs of interaction; such costs may include the effort of learning how the other person will behave, and learning what behaviour will be acceptable to the other. In addition, predictability may also involve knowing how to elicit rewarding behaviour from one's partner. In all, once such achievements have been made, the outcome of the relationship will be greater, making it more likely to be higher than the CLalt., and so less likely to be abandoned in favour of another relationship.

A final stage in the development of relationships is *institutionalization* in which norms are developed to recognize the legitimacy of the particular form of relationship and patterns of rewards and costs which have evolved within it. Not all relationships result in institutionalization, or even in commitment, although a typical example of one which does is marriage. Others may not have a formal legal procedure for institutionalization, but may have a symbolic acknowledgment, such as the exchange of rings by engaged couples, or even a recognition of friendship by cutting fingers and mingling blood.

Another branch of research applicable to interpersonal attraction, which has been explained in terms of exchange theory, is that which supports the notion that two people may be attracted to each other because each has personality characteristics, or needs, which the other can complement, so that both partners find mutual satisfaction. Winch (1958) in his 'complementary needs hypothesis' proposed that mate selection is a process whereby the individuals involved are seeking to find a partner who will supply some deficiency in themselves, so that, ideally, each has a need which the other will satisfy. As a result of a factor analytic study investigating needs (Murray, 1938) of married couples, Winch concluded that there are bipolar dimensions of mate selection which can be described by needs and traits which are nurturant–receptive, and dominant–submissive such that receptive individuals tend to select those who are nurturant and *vice versa*. Similarly, dominant individuals tend to select a spouse who is submissive.

Winch's study is considerably more detailed than has been described, and forms a large part of the research on complementary needs, suggesting that within an interpersonal relationship, such as marriage, the needs of one partner are satisfied by traits in the other, so that, in terms of exchange theory, one partner is rewarded at a slight cost (the behaviour by which the trait is manifest) to the other. Similar conclusions, with different subject populations, have been reached by Bermann and Miller (1967) using student nurses, Hilkevitch (1960) using schoolboy friendships, Kerchoff and Davis (1962) using dating couples, and Swensen (1967) using psychotherapists and their clients.

However, a fair amount of research has not supported the notion of complementarity of needs in interpersonal relationships (e.g. Bowerman and Day, 1965; Izard, 1960; Murstein, 1961); the major finding of such studies has been that it is similarity of traits, rather than their complementarity, which makes for a successful interpersonal relationship. A further problem for research based on the complementary needs hypothesis is that it has used rather unusual subject samples. Winch, for example, drew his subjects from married couples at least one of whom was an undergraduate student at a particular American university; all were white, middle-class, American born, childless, aged between nineteen and twenty-six, and married for less than two years. Such criticisms, and research indicating contrary trends, perhaps imply that the complementary needs hypothesis has provided ample stimulus for research but has not been adequately demonstrated. It may be that convincing support is yet to be found. If this is not the case, it could be argued that there is little damage to exchange theory, since an individual may complement his traits and needs outside the marriage relationship (or, alternatively, outside whatever relationship the experimenter who has failed to find support has chosen to observe).

(c) *How adequate is exchange theory?*

The advantages of exchange theory are relatively obvious: it is a theory of social behaviour which has been well rooted within a strong experimental psychological tradition, renowned for its hard-headed, no-nonsense approach. This may be part of its appeal to social psychologists who are often told that theirs is the 'soft' area of the discipline. In addition, its tenets seem, intuitively, to be right: an interpersonal relationship does cost, and the rewards it produces generally outweigh the costs. Further undoubted advantages of the theory are that it examines interactions between individuals, rather than the behaviour of single subjects; that the four-stage model is concerned with the development of a relationship; and that it is able to explain many aspects of social behaviour, attraction being a small part of its domain, and it therefore unites different types of behaviours within a common framework.

On the less favourable side, critics have argued that exchange theory cannot really explain behaviour that may come within certain domains, for example, altruism. Sacrifices made by one human being for another are difficult to interpret in terms of a reward–cost outcome. This may seem a sentimental and unscientific criticism, and indeed Homans (1961) attempts to deal with this problem by claiming that there are many types of profit which may depend on a variety of values. Altruistic behaviour, according to exchange theory, therefore depends on individuals valuing themselves as humanitarians, or as devoted parents or lovers, and as being rewarded for behaving as such. There are various problems with this. First, it may not be the most parsimonious explanation; second, it implies that by invoking a notion of a humanitarian value, one is making a retrospective explanation which is scarcely in line with the behaviourist tradition on which the theory prides itself. Finally, if it is acceptable to invoke new values to account for reward when the theory runs into difficulties, then it cannot be disproved by any type of experiment. This is not the hallmark of a scientific theory.

10 Conclusion: consistency or reinforcement for attraction?

Work discussed in this chapter indicates that consistency theories of attraction have a fair amount of support, whereas theories based on reinforcement principles are less viable. Before reconsidering this conclusion, it may be worth making some more general points about psychological studies of attraction.

It could be argued that this chapter has dealt with an area of social psychology which is of crucial importance for everyday life. Nevertheless much of the research appears artificial and contrived. Indeed, with the exception of the studies by Newcomb (e.g. 1943; 1956) and Duck (e.g. 1973, 1977) and Duck and Craig (1978) one is often confronted by research attempting to demonstrate attraction where it cannot, in its normal sense, be present.

A further point can be made as a general criticism of all the theories considered. They offer little in the way of explanation for attraction. Consistency theories, it could be argued, merely describe the results of similarity of attitude. Byrne's (1961a) reinforcement theory proposes that the basis of agreement is reinforcement, but perhaps this only states the obvious. Considering these points there can be little surprise when psychologists from outside this field infer that we know little about this crucial area of human relationships.

When considering the various theories that have been discussed, that of Newcomb (1953) appears to be soundest, theoretically and experimentally. In addition, when Heider's (1958) theory of dyadic balance can be tested (there are problems due to the interpretation of the negative relation as ambivalent), the data is often supportive. Research on factors such as physical attractiveness and propinquity can also be seen within a consistency framework if one accepts that they form a good *Gestalt* with interpersonal attraction and therefore a consistent, or balanced situation.

The remaining theories considered in relation to attraction have been Byrne's (1961a) reinforcement theory, and social exchange theory (e.g. Thibaut and Kelley, 1959). There is less support for these theories, for reasons which relate to the particular theories rather than to their both being rooted within behaviourist psychology. One of the tenets of Byrne's theory is that agreement is rewarding because it provides consensual validation of one's attitudes. This point, though crucial to the theory, has been difficult to demonstrate. In addition, the experimental paradigm Byrne uses makes one question its relevance to real life friendships, and to question similarly the relevance of his theory. Social exchange theory, although based in a similar tradition, is more widely applicable to different areas of social behaviour. There are, however, problems with its reward–cost explanation in that when data are not supportive it is easy to posit that a subject has a particular value or need which is somehow rewarded. As such it is a theory which is incapable of disproof, and cannot therefore be seen as scientific (Popper, 1959).

Of the consistency theories discussed in this chapter, Newcomb's is the most successful. In comparing this with the theories based on reinforcement principles it can be seen, again, that consistency is the better supported principle. For example, Newcomb and Byrne predict very similar predictions, though claim a different theoretical basis. However, the essential difference – Byrne's claim that positive affect accrues to the person with whom one validates one's attitudes – has not been demonstrated convincingly. A further difference is that Newcomb (1956) emphasizes the relevance or importance of the issue on which there is agreement or disagreement; he is supported in this by the results of Rodrigues (1965) and of Zajonc and Burnstein (1965). Byrne, however, maintains that attraction is a function of the proportion of attitudes on which two people agree. This seems intuitively unlikely in anything other than the particular experimental paradigm which Byrne adopts. Normally, one does not have a checklist of attitudinal issues to be used when meeting a stranger! It seems more likely that important agreements and disagreements affect attraction, and unimportant ones do not.

It is more difficult to compare the theory of interpersonal communication with social exchange theory, since they have few areas of similarity. Social exchange is more applicable to wider areas of behaviour, but is theoretically weak. It appears that neither theory of interpersonal attraction based on reinforcement principles represents a serious challenge to consistency theories.

5 Group influences on judgmental decisions

To some extent one might consider that all social psychology is the study of how groups influence individual behaviour, and it may therefore seem a little extraordinary that a chapter concerned with group influences should be towards the end of this book, rather than at the beginning. However, this chapter will not deal with the majority of group processes which have been studied by social psychologists. For example, roles, status, social power, and leadership have all been popular topics for study, but have not been primarily related to cognitive processes, and will therefore not be included in this book. (For a discussion of such group processes see, for example, Secord and Backman, 1974.) In this chapter we are more concerned with the way membership of a group affects the types of phenomena that have been described in earlier chapters, such as judgments on attitudinal issues or personal characteristics.

An immediate question which may follow is the problem of what constitutes a group. Baron, Byrne and Griffitt (1974) suggest that a collection of individuals can only be considered to be a group if they experience a sense of belonging with each other; if they share goals, values, beliefs and interests, and if the fates of the individuals are interdependent. While these may seem quite reasonable criteria, social psychologists have not always followed them when performing experiments on groups. It is sometimes the case that collections of unrelated strangers are brought together to perform an experimental task. It may be that during the task a sense of groupness emerges, and that, being drawn from a common population, subjects do share many values and beliefs. Nevertheless, these characteristics may not be apparent at the beginning of the experiment. Some of the work to be discussed – the 'minimal group experiments' (e.g. Tajfel, Flament, Billig and Bundy, 1971) are partly an attempt to establish the conditions necessary for subjects to feel that they belong to a group.

The topics to be dealt with in this chapter include intra-group influences on individual decision making, and the way group membership has been seen to influence an individual's decisions about his own and other groups. The latter will be discussed under the topic of inter-group discrimination, and includes theories of prejudice, and the work beginning with the 'minimal group experiments' (e.g. Tajfel, Flament, Billig and Bundy, 1971) and leading to Tajfel's (1978) theory of intergroup behaviour. Finally, the phenomenon which has come to be called 'group polarization' (also termed 'risky shift', 'choice shifts', or 'group extremization') will be considered. This is concerned with the way individuals come to make a joint group decision, and may be partially explained in terms of the topics discussed earlier in the chapter.

I Intra-group influences

Most of the studies concerned with the way a group influences one of its members have dealt with how the individual member conforms to the group norms. In this sense, a norm is 'an expectation shared by group members which specifies behaviour that is considered appropriate for a given situation' (Secord and Backman, 1974, p.300). As such, a variety of behaviours can be considered normative: for example, the amorphous group of British road users considers it normative that vehicles should move on the left of the road, and anyone driving on the right would be considered deviant and would hastily be required to conform. More intimate groups have norms that may be known only to their members: for example, secret societies may have particular forms of handshake or greeting.

While it is relatively easy to find examples of norms or

expectations shared by group members, how they have developed is less obvious. One of the earliest demonstrations of this was given by Sherif in 1935 using the autokinetic phenomenon. This is an effect in which a stationary point of light, if shown repeatedly against a dark background so that there is no frame of reference, will appear to move. As there are no visual cues on which to base judgments, subjects who are asked to estimate the distance through which the light has moved tend to use each others' estimates for guidance. In Sherif's experiment there were two conditions. In the first, subjects made individual judgments, and were then brought together as a group, in which the judgments were made again. In the group session, subjects modified their initial judgments so as to lessen the discrepancy between their own and the judgments of other group members. In the second condition the order of the sessions was reversed, and a norm was established in the group session which then affected judgments made in the individual session. This persistent norm is all the more interesting in that subjects appeared to be unaware of the group's influence on their judgments. It seems that we may not realize that we are influenced by norms, and that the influence can persist outside the situation in which they were developed. It is easy to see how the experience of everyday life concords with this.

Later work has qualified Sherif's original study showing that subjects are more likely to be influenced by each other when they are friends rather than strangers (Pollis, 1967; Pollis and Montgomery, 1968): when another subject, actually a stooge, forms an unbalanced situation (see Chapter 2) (Sampson and Insko, 1964): and when subjects were led to believe that the light really would move, as compared to a condition in which they were told that the apparent movement was an illusion (Alexander, Zucker and Brody, 1970).

A further classic experiment concerned with intra-group influence is that of Asch (1956), which differed in its essential paradigm from the Sherif study, but more importantly, used an unambiguous situation in which the judgmental decision was apparently obvious. Subjects were grouped with a number of stooges, usually about seven, and all were seated in front of a screen on which lines of varying length were presented. The task for the subjects was to choose a line which was of the same length as the standard, a judgment which was totally obvious. However, on two thirds of the trials subjects found that those responding before them, who were all confederates, unanimously made incorrect judgments. Most of the subjects yielded to this group pressure by conforming to the obviously wrong decision made by the rest of the group, at least on some of the trials.

The work of both Sherif and Asch poses an important question. Why is it that subjects are so readily influenced by other members of a group, even when they have information that the rest of the group have made inaccurate judgments? One way of answering this question is in terms of Festinger's (1950) suggestion that we have a need to evaluate our opinions. This can either be done by recourse to physical reality or by using social reality. Very often we use our physical senses to check our beliefs (e.g. Is there really a magpie on the lawn?). However, only certain sorts of information are capable of being checked by physical reality. Many of our beliefs are founded in social reality, and we need other people's opinions to validate our own. For example, 'I believe Communists are thoroughly evil, don't you?' is more than a statement of one's own and question about another's opinions. It is more of a request for agreement and confirmation on an issue which may be fundamental to one's own self concept. Disagreement can lead to doubt about one's interpretation of the social world, and therefore about one's own standing in it. Furthermore, such information can only be validated by reliance on other people's opinions. When a stimulus to be judged is totally unambiguous, and it can be assessed by one's physical senses, there is really little need to rely on social reality.

In the Asch study, although this appeared to be the case, subjects may possibly have doubted their own eyesight on listening to others unanimously making apparently incorrect judgments. Alternatively, they may have thought that they misunderstood the task. Believing themselves to be wrong, the subjects had no alternative but to accept the others' judgments, thus anchoring their own in social reality. In the Sherif study, no accurate judgment of the movement of the light could be made (since the light was stationary), so that the situation was an ambiguous one in which different subjects made different decisions. It is in just such situations that subjects are forced to rely on social reality and thus conform to a 'group decision'.

While the studies mentioned above are, of course, classics in the social psychology of groups, and conformity is an important tendency in social behaviour, it is by no means the only influence which members of a group can exert on each other. The opposite tendency may be termed deviance or innovation, perhaps depending on which evaluation one wishes to place on the behaviour. (For a detailed discussion of deviance see Secord and Backman, 1974.) Moscovici (1976) and Moscovici and Lage (1976) have been concerned with mechanisms underlying innovation, and how it differs from conformity. Moscovici suggests that a deviant *may* be regarded as a person who rejects group influence and attempts to have his own opinions adopted by the group. Alternatively such behaviour may result from a need to distinguish oneself from others and to assert what is believed to be important.

Moscovici and Lage (1976) provided an ingenious experimental demonstration of the way innovation differs from conformity. Subjects in an Asch-type situation were asked to view a number of slides projected on to a screen. All the subjects and the confederates were first given a colour vision test so as to demonstrate to each other that none of them had defective colour vision. They were then asked to name the colour of each of the slides. Each slide was in fact the same colour although the light intensity varied from slide to slide. The colour was such as to be called 'blue' by the control group, a response which Moscovici and Lage term a 'cultural truism' (p.149), although the response 'green' was plausible but rare. In different experimental conditions the number of confederates and their behaviour varied. Thus a consistent minority (two confederates with a group of four subjects) made the deviant response ('green') in one condition, whereas in another, the two confederates were inconsistent, sometimes responding 'green' and sometimes 'blue'. In a further condition a single confederate consistently responded 'green'.

In the majority conditions the confederates always responded 'green' and were in a majority within the group. Finally, in a control group, subjects made their responses in writing and were not influenced by confederates. Following these experimental manipulations a further interesting measure was taken; subjects were given a colour discrimination test as an investigation of their latent responses, thus showing whether any influence, caused by the confederates in the initial part of the experiment, had any lasting effect. Finally, a post experimental questionnaire investigated how subjects perceived the confederates and the interpersonal relationships within the group.

The data from this experiment indicated that innovation and conformity may be radically different processes such that conformity to the majority of the group affects only those responses made in the group situation, there being no changes in the latent responses, implying that conformity is a superficial effect and not one that changes real opinions. Innovation, however, takes place when there is a consistent minority of more than one individual, and such influence affects latent as well as manifest responses. It appears, then, that innovation is a more powerful effect, caused by the consistent and coherent responses of a minority of individuals. According to Moscovici and Lage it is this behavioural style which affects the interaction within the group, causing members to respect the views of the minority. As such the minority's influence is by way of persuasion, rather than by authority or through a need for affiliation. The majority, however, produces different intra-group relations, causing influence by its apparent competence and assurance, and being less attractive than a consistent minority.

The work by Moscovici and Lage which has just been described essentially implies that conformity and innovation are different processes and not opposite poles of a tendency to comply with group norms. The same conclusion can be made from a rather different body of work, looking at the position of the deviant or innovator within the group. Lemaine (1974) argues that group members must find themselves a 'vacant place' (p.18) within the group where they can offer something different from other members and where their position will be valued. To some extent this has been demonstrated experimentally by Codol (1975) who shows that an individual attempts to distinguish himself from the rest of the group, but, above all, tends to see his own behaviour as more normative than that of other members. Thus, according to Codol, an individual believes himself to be closer to both the group's ideals and standards of behaviour and to its conventions than are other members. This so-called 'superior conformity of the self' implies that individuals value their group membership, and yet at the same time they attempt to find themselves a 'vacant place' within the group. This behaviour may well be that of the innovator, and in no way complies with the traditional conformity model which suggests that group norms are followed in order to be accepted by the rest of the group.

It thus appears that much of the early work concerned with intra-group influences, only a small sample of which has been discussed here, has seen these influences in terms of control and compliance. More recently the behaviour of the individual within the group has been considered in greater detail, with the suggestion that when the proposals of a minority are consistent then they may be a powerful agent of influence. Again it appears that consistency is an important tendency causing predictable, and therefore respected and influential, behaviour.

2 Inter-group discrimination

A common criticism of social psychology is that, although it purports to be concerned with the way people influence and interact with each other, many of the studies used to investigate its subject matter are either approaching the bizarre, having little in common with everyday social behaviour (see, for example Ring, 1967) or else appear to be interested in solitary aspects of human behaviour. The former criticism might be levelled at some of the experiments already described in this chapter: how often, the sceptic could ask, do we attempt to change our friends' perceptions of blue to green, or to ask them to make judgments about the lengths of lines, particularly when the answer is obvious anyway? Some of the studies to be described in this section are subject to the same criticism, while others seem to have lost the social part of their subject matter. In defence of such studies it has to be said that experimenters often need to simplify the phenomena in which they are interested so as to remove extraneous events and to allow the methodology to be suitable for the laboratory. It may be, of course, that in doing so they have radically changed the phenomenon in which they were initially interested (see, for example, Tajfel, 1972). Many of the studies concerned with inter-group discrimination have intentionally simplified the situation in which subjects find themselves, to the extent that there is no social interaction between them, in order to demonstrate that the mere perception of a difference between groups is sufficient to lead to discrimination (e.g. Tajfel, Flament, Billig and Bundy, 1971; Billig and Tajfel, 1973). Cognitive social psychologists argue, therefore, that such perceptions are very much their concern, even though subjects in the experiments underwent a somewhat asocial experience.

Much of the work to be discussed in this section stems from Tajfel and his co-workers and can be divided into that concerned with the 'minimal group experiments' (e.g. Tajfel *et al*, 1971), that concerned with real groups (e.g. Doise and Sinclair, 1973; Branthwaite and Jones, 1975; Turner, 1978), and Tajfel's (1978) theory of inter-group behaviour. Much of this work is applicable to a cognitive explanation of prejudice, and it is theories of prejudice with which the discussion will begin.

(a) *Theories of prejudice*

(i) *The authoritarian personality*

Probably the best known explanation of prejudice comes from Adorno, Frenkel-Brunswick, Levinson and Sanford (1950) in their classic study known as *The Authoritarian Personality*. This study, carried out in the late 1940s was exceptional, not only in its influence on later psychology, but in its relevance to the current social issues. The hypothesis of the study was that people who are anti-semitic will hold additional attitudes which are not obviously related, but can be shown to be so through investigation of the subject's personality structure. Adorno *et al.* demonstrated that those with highly anti-semitic attitudes were also ethnocentric and had a tendency to political and economic conservatism. This cluster of antagonistic attitudes towards Jews and other minority groups tends to be associated with a resistance to social change, and, in addition, is related to a potentiality for fascism. The latter, measured by the so-called 'F scale', was claimed to be a personality dimension which caused the subject to be susceptible to fascist propaganda.

Adorno *et al.* collected data by using attitude and personality scales, and by interviews and projective tests. They interpreted the relationship between attitudes and personality in terms of Freudian theory. Subjects who were high on the F scale, and also on the anti-semitic and ethnocentrism scales, described their parents, in interview, in idealized terms, and as having been very strict. The authors proposed that such descriptions must denote an intolerance of ambivalent feelings towards parents, and hence a repression of the negative aspects of those feelings, on the part of prejudiced subjects, since the descriptions were improbably positive and idealized. It was further argued that the repressed negative feelings were projected on to Jews and other minority groups who thus acted as a kind of scapegoat. In addition, parents of prejudiced subjects were described as having been anxious about status and having dealt with their children in an authoritarian manner. Adorno *et al.* reasoned that discipline would have frustrated the children thus causing aggression according to the frustration–aggression hypothesis (Dollard, Doob, Miller, Mowrer and Sears, 1939). Since the aggression could not be directed against the parents, for fear of reprisal, it was displaced on to minority groups and Jews.

The Authoritarian Personality may be criticized on a number of grounds. First, as it uses the Freudian defence mechanisms repression, projection and displacement, it must be subject to many of the criticisms levelled at Freud for describing and using unscientific concepts (see, for example, Eysenck and Wilson, 1973). Even if one holds that Freud never intended his concepts to be rigorously testable in a scientific manner, Adorno *et al.* surely adopted them as such and can therefore be criticized in this way. Apart from such problems of a theoretical nature, the study has been attacked on methodological grounds. Hyman and Sheatsley (1954), for example, claim that the questionnaire data on which the attitude measures were collected were not controlled for response set. It was further suggested that the subjects in the study were not a representative sample of any specifiable population, even though it was proposed that the results could be generalized to white, non-Jewish, native-born, middle-class Americans. A further serious problem is that, at the time of the interview, interviewers were aware of subjects' responses on the attitude and personality scales so that, according to Adorno *et al.*, they might be guided in the questions they asked. However, knowledge of whether they were dealing with a prejudiced or unprejudiced subject may well have led interviewers to probe in particular areas to obtain evidence of, for example, strict or idealized parents.

In spite of these serious criticisms, *The Authoritarian Personality* has been extremely influential in psychology in the years following its publication. Subsequent studies (Christie and Cook, 1958) have confirmed its major findings, and, regardless of its methodological flaws, the relationship it proposes remains an intriguing explanation of prejudice.

(ii) *Vicarious classical conditioning*

A further explanation of prejudice, though more limited in its scope, has been proposed by Baron, Byrne and Griffitt (1974), using vicarious classical conditioning as the method by which a person comes to learn intolerant attitudes. According to this process, a neutral stimulus which is initially incapable of eliciting strong emotional responses from observers acquires the ability to do so when it is repeatedly seen with signs of emotional reaction from those on whom the observers may be modelling their behaviour (see, for example, Berger, 1962). Baron *et al.* suggest that this process would account for the development of prejudice in children if a child observes his parent showing signs of anger or disgust in the presence of a member of a particular racial group. Such reactions will lead to the arousal of similar emotions in the child by vicarious emotional arousal in the presence of the parent, and after repeated occasions, in the absence of the parent, by vicarious classical conditioning. The final process, suggested by Baron *et al.*, is for the child to add cognitions to his emotional reactions ('I hate Jews because they are always out to make money'), so resulting in the prejudice portrayed by adults.

While this seems a very plausible explanation as far as it goes, it cannot be regarded as the complete picture. Why, for example, were the child's parents prejudiced? It seems that vicarious classical conditioning is adequate to explain the transmission, but not the initiation, of prejudice.

(iii) *A cognitive approach to prejudice*

A more thorough-going explanation has been provided by Tajfel (1969) through a cognitive approach to prejudice and stereotypes. According to this view an important aspect of the phenomenon is the tendency to react to members of an outgroup (i.e. a particular racial or national group which is not one's own) in terms of group membership and without regard to individual differences within the group.

Such a prediction was made by Tajfel and Wilkes (1963) and has support in the field of interpersonal judgments. For example, Secord, Bevan and Katz (1956) and Secord (1959) showed that the degree of stereotyping was greater for prejudiced subjects when judging photographs which varied from highly Negroid to highly Caucasian. Stereotyped personality traits were assigned to photographs which were recognized as being Negroid regardless of the extent to which they actually contained Caucasian features. It appears that once a prejudiced subject has categorized a person as Negro, the stereotypes which he attaches to this label will also be attributed to the person. A similar conclusion can be drawn from a study by Tajfel, Sheikh and Gardner (1964) in which subjects rated two Indians and two Canadians on a number of bipolar dimensions. Some of the dimensions used formed part of the stereotype of Indians while others were unrelated. Similarly, some dimensions formed part of the Canadian stereotype while others did not. The Indians and Canadians were interviewed in front of the subjects who then gave their ratings. Tajfel *et al.* showed that the two Indians were rated as more similar to each other on dimensions forming part of the stereotype than on those which were unrelated. An analogous result was obtained for the Canadian ratings, demonstrating that the differences between members of an ethnic group are minimized on traits which are thought to characterize that group.

According to Tajfel (1969) this tendency on the part of prejudiced subjects to categorize individuals into their ethnic groups is only one of a series of cognitive aspects of prejudice. Additional processes include assimilation and coherence. In the former an individual assimilates the norms and values of his society so that he learns evaluations about his own and other groups and identifies with his own ethnic or cultural group. There is evidence from Goodman (1964) that, at least in a highly prejudiced society, children may do this as early as three or four years of age. The process of coherence allows the individual to build a consistent cognitive structure to explain his evaluations in terms of ethnic groups. Tajfel's example of the child who maintained that he did not like Russians because Hitler was their chief demonstrates how consistency may be used in a cognitive structure in order to preserve the individual's self image and explain (at least at one level) his prejudice.

Tajfel's cognitive explanation of prejudice is in many respects preferable to those previously discussed. He sees prejudice as an adaptive function of man in the senses that it reduces the amount of information which an individual is required to process and that it maximizes the possibility of positive self esteem, even though it may have disastrous consequences. In addition, what Tajfel has proposed is a complete and easily testable explanation, and one which already has a fair amount of empirical support.

(b) *Minimal conditions for inter-group discrimination*

The explanations of prejudice considered in the previous section address themselves directly to an obvious and fundamental social problem. This is not so with the studies to be reported in this section, which is concerned with experiments aimed at discovering the minimal conditions necessary for subjects to exhibit discrimination between their own and other groups. As such, the experiments are concerned with issues similar to those discussed in the previous section, although the approach to these issues is more indirect.

An early series of studies on this problem was carried out by Sherif (see Sherif, 1951; 1966; Sherif and Sherif 1953), using boys in a summer camp as subjects. These studies were concerned with the effect of dividing the boys into two competing groups and the ways in which their behaviour was altered by this division were investigated. It was shown that even if group division cut across existing friendship bands it exerted a powerful influence on subsequent perceptions of the subject's own group (or in-group) and the rival group (or out-group). Each group developed its own separate hierarchy and culture and showed strong overt hostility towards the out-group, particularly in sporting activities.

An experiment by Blake and Mouton (1962) extended this work. Forty-eight groups were involved, competing in pairs, triads or quartets, to solve a business management problem. Over 92 per cent of the subjects found their own group's solution superior to that of other groups, a result which was attributed to individuals believing that their own capacities were reflected in the group decision and were being evaluated. In judging the various solutions offered, it appeared that groups used a kind of perceptual distortion by using dimensions which presented their own solutions in a positive light. Positive qualities of other solutions appeared less relevant.

Rabbie and Horwitz (1969) extended this early work on the minimal conditions required for group discrimination by testing Lewin's (1948) hypothesis that the main criterion for feeling that one belongs to a group is interdependence of fate with other group members. Groups of eight subjects were divided into two equal sub-groups and performed in one of four experimental conditions, which were introduced after some preliminary tasks. In three conditions rewards (transistor radios) were obtained by the members of one group, the experimenter announcing that he did not have sufficient to give rewards to both groups. In one condition the reward was obtained by one group by chance, in another by the experimenter's choice of group, and in the third by the group's effort. In a final, control, condition there was no reward at stake. As the dependent variable, subjects rated their impressions of others in their session. The results showed that there was no in-group bias in the control condition, but in the remaining three conditions, in which subjects were rewarded, more favourable ratings were given to members of the in-group.

Rabbie and Horwitz concluded that only when group members experienced common fate would in-group bias occur, both groups feeling a common emotional bond due to success or failure. Since this did not occur in the control group, the authors concluded that group classification, in itself, is insufficient to produce discrimination. However, the control subjects had been arbitrarily divided into the two groups, had worked separately at different tasks and were then asked to rate members of their own and the other group on the same personality characteristics as used in the other conditions. It is arguable, therefore, that the classification in the control group was not seen as relevant, and that these subjects may not have perceived themselves as members of one or other sub-group at all.

This experiment was criticized by Tajfel, Flament, Billig and Bundy (1971) who claimed that the task allotted to the control subjects was meaningless and contrived and therefore the classification into sub-groups was unlikely to elicit in-group bias. It could not, therefore be considered a test of the minimal conditions necessary for group discrimination.

Tajfel *et al.* conducted two experiments, which with further studies from Tajfel and his co-workers (e.g. Billig and Tajfel, 1973; Tajfel and Billig, 1974) have been termed the 'minimal group experiments', and were specifically designed to find the minimal conditions for inter-group discrimination. The experimental groups in these studies have none of the characteristics normally associated with group interaction and discrimination. There is no face-to-face interaction between any of the subjects, and group membership is anonymous. Further, there is no rational link between the criteria for group membership and the type of in-group-out-group discriminatory responses, and these responses do not represent any value to the subject making them. For example, a subject is never able to allocate money or points to himself. In addition, the strategy of responding in terms of the in-group-out-group bias is in opposition to that based on rational or utilitarian principles such as maximum benefit for all. Finally, Tajfel *et al.* suggested that responses should be important to the subjects in that they should be real decisions about real rewards, rather than evaluation of others on, for example, personality traits.

In the initial experiment reported, subjects were schoolboys aged 14-15 years and were first asked to take part in a guessing task. A series of dots were flashed up on to a screen and subjects estimated the number of dots on each side. They were then divided into two groups, allegedly on the basis of their estimations, but in fact randomly. The final task was to allot money to their fellow subjects; they were to know which group they themselves were in, but not the identity of other group members. In no case was a subject able to allot money to himself, and nor was he aware of the identity of any of those to whom he was awarding money, except for their group membership. The money could be allotted in a number of separate assignments each of which involved a comparative choice between two boys, each a member of a different group. This initial experiment showed consistent in-group bias: with no knowledge of other group members, no anticipated interaction or competition, and no recognized value associated with group membership, subjects still preferred their own group.

The second experiment used a different task to divide subjects into two groups. Subjects looked at pairs of slides of paintings by Klee and Kandinsky, recorded a preference for one of each pair, and were divided into groups according to their apparent preference for one or other painter. Following this division, similar anonymity conditions were used as in the initial experiment and subjects were asked to allot money to members of their own and the other group. This was done using a set of matrices so designed that they could distinguish between the following three types of response strategy:

1 'Maximum joint profit': subjects awarding money so that maximum benefit for both groups was obtained.
2 'Maximum in-group profit': subjects awarding money so as to maximize the individual outcomes of the member of the subject's own group.
3 'Maximum difference': subjects awarding money so as to give the maximum difference between that allotted to the two others, to the advantage of the in-group member.

The results of this study were similar to that of the previous one in that there was a marked preference for in-group favouritism, even when this reduced the maximum benefit and resulted in a reduced absolute award for in-group members. Subjects sought the maximum difference between in-group and out-group members, rather than the maximum possible profit for the in-group.

In answer to possible criticisms of artificiality and strangeness in the experiment, Tajfel and Billig (1974) argued that subjects might be more likely to use group divisions when uncertain of the task, and thus inter-group discrimination would be less marked if subjects were familiar with the procedure. In this experiment half of the subjects were familiarized with the setting and task before the critical session. Both the familiar and the naive subjects showed in-group favouritism and used the maximum difference strategy, but contrary to predictions, inter-group discrimination increased with task familiarity. It is clearly not the unusual nature of the experiment which is responsible for in-group bias.

A further experiment in this series (Billig and Tajfel, 1973) sought to differentiate between categorization and perceived similarity in terms of an attribute (i.e. preference for a particular painter) which subjects might well believe the experimenters deemed important. It might be that similarity, perhaps through interpersonal attraction (e.g. Newcomb, 1961), causes in-group bias. An experiment was performed in which subjects were divided either into distinct categories, or into loose divisions distinguishable only by different code numbers. Categorization into groups produced a stronger in-group bias than the similarity variable, and it appeared that categorization has an effect which is not attributable to similarity.

To summarize this series of experiments, it appears that a simple classification into groups according to an apparently meaningless and value-free criterion results in group members seeking maximum differentiation between their own and the other group. This tendency is increased by familiarization with the task, and does not depend on the classification being on the grounds of similarity of some attribute. The experiments showed that activity within or between groups is not required to produce inter-group discrimination; nevertheless such interaction and explicit competition between groups might well enhance the effect.

Before discussing the function of these experiments and the effect they demonstrate, it is as well to consider a criticism made of the 'minimal group' studies. In particular, Gerard and Hoyt (1974) have argued that subjects are put in a forced choice situation, having to favour one or other group and having only the group classification on which to base their decisions. This criticism is inept, since the response matrices were designed so as to allow subjects to allocate money according to strategies of maximum joint profit, fairness, or in-group bias. Implicit in the Gerard and Hoyt criticism is the notion that the 'minimal group studies' can be explained by the experimenter effect (e.g. Orne, 1962). However, Tajfel *et al.* argued that although this may have been an important aspect of the situation, it in no way provides an explanation of the results.

> The point of the experiments was to activate for the Ss the norm of 'groupness' under certain specified conditions .... What does seem theoretically important is the fact that a few references to 'groupness' in the instructions were sufficient to release the kind of behaviour that was observed despite its 'non-rational' ... character, despite the

> flimsy criteria for social categorization .., and despite the possibility of using alternative and in some ways 'better' strategies. (Tajfel *et al.*, 1971, p.174)

Having discussed the minimal conditions necessary for inter-group discrimination, and in particular detail the 'minimal group' experiments, it is worth considering why the notion of 'group' is so important for producing discriminatory behaviour. The most adequate explanation has been given by Turner (1975); it uses the concepts of social identity and social comparison. According to Turner, subjects in an experiment are faced with having to make sense of what is happening, and indeed this is so of anyone in any unfamiliar situation. In an inter-group situation a person has to define his social identity, that is, to compare himself in relation to others, and the initial explanation holds that social categorization provides a framework for this comparison so that a person can compare his own group with others.

Turner uses Festinger's (1954) notion of social comparison, a term which describes the process in which a person engages when he is unsure of his standing on non-objective criteria. Thus a person compares himself with others to give himself a comparative measure when there is no other 'objective' way of establishing reality. According to Turner, members of a group use social comparison in the inter-group situation so comparing their group with the out-group in order to establish positive social identity. To do this, a person wishes to compare himself favourably with others, and this will be possible for him if he is a member of a group which can prove itself 'better' on some dimension than is another group. The group and the dimension thus become salient to his self-concept and social identity.

In the 'minimal group' situation, therefore, subjects are faced with a relatively novel state of affairs which they wish to make sense of. In doing so they will use a social comparison process which enables them to maintain positive social identity. Since the situation is so 'minimal' this necessitates comparison of their own group with the out-group on the only dimension the experiment allows.

The conclusions to be drawn, then, from the minimal

group experiments are, firstly, that inter-group discrimination can be produced by separating subjects into meaningless or arbitrary divisions (one might suppose that it is very likely that with more meaningful groups discrimination will be greater), and, secondly, that this social categorization leads to social comparison in order to obtain a positive social identity.

A third, rather more speculative, inference comes from Billig (1976) who suggests that the 'minimal group' experiments demonstrate the power of social labels in society. Such real-life labels, for example Jews–Gentiles or middle class–working class, are linguistic categories. Members of these categories, however, do not share everything in common, and there is no overall assumption of absolute similarity between members of such groups. Billig maintains that nevertheless language gives the impression that the classification is much neater than it really is. For example, by referring to the middle class in comparison with the working class one ignores many individuals who might fall into one category on one occasion but into another with a different classificatory system. In addition to tidying up a messy classification, the existence of such labels allows members of the category to identify with their category. Thus, in the same way as subjects in the 'minimal group' experiments could identify with, for instance, the group preferring Klee, so a Jewish person can identify with the Jews, even though this is really a group of widely differing people, separated historically and geographically.

Billig further proposes that one can adapt the Marxist concept of false consciousness to explain the 'minimal group' studies. This concept claims that the ideology of the dominant group shapes that of the subordinate group in society. According to this Marxist analysis, the ideology of the subordinate group (for example, the working class) is determined by and for the dominant middle class, so that the objective conditions of society are concealed, and so that the dominant group can maintain its superiority. According to Billig this tendency is aided by the social categorization effect, labels such as 'working class' helping the formation of a false consciousness.

This interpretation draws upon the 'minimal group' experiments in arguing that social categorization divides a continuum into psychologically separate entities and exaggerates the differences between them. These experiments also show, Billig claims, the power of a prestigious authority, for example the experimenter, or the dominant group in society, to create groups or categories. Their acceptance by subjects, or by society, represents a false consciousness which hides the objective conditions of the situation. In essence, then, the inference is that these experiments demonstrate how social labels can perpetuate conditions favouring one group in society.

It was suggested earlier in this chapter that some of the studies relating to inter-group discrimination were performed in an apparently indirect and asocial manner. This was not meant as a criticism, but merely pointed out that social behaviour must often be simplified in experiments, if a psychologist is to discover its roots or minimal causes. This is the case with the 'minimal group' experiments, and any claim that they have been so simplified that they no longer provide a relevant social situation, must be considered in the light of the inference drawn from them by Billig. If Billig's analysis is accepted, then these experiments may be some of the most socially relevant studies discussed in this book.

(c) *Discrimination between real groups*

A small number of studies have adapted the theoretical and in some cases methodological approaches, discussed above, to investigate discrimination between real groups. Some of these studies will be briefly considered in this section. In many cases real groups which are the focus of discrimination are seen as inferior in some aspect by the group doing the discriminating. One attempt to mimic this condition in the laboratory was by Turner (1978) who asked groups of either Science or Arts students to rewrite a passage of prose so as to improve its clarity and style; subjects were instructed that Arts students were definitely superior to Science students in verbal intelligence (stable condition) or that verbal intelligence was more important for Arts than Science students (unstable condition). Ratings were obtained of the respective merits of the two groups' performances (by having subjects rate their own and the other group's performance), and of subjects' preferences for being a member of their own or the other group. The results suggested that groups in a position of unstable superiority discriminate more than those in a position of stable superiority. However, it must be remembered that the superiority manipulation was by instructions given to the subjects, and although relevant to the experimental task, may have been irrelevant to their self perceptions.

An experiment using a socially rather than experimentally defined inequality between groups was carried out by Doise and Sinclair (1973) who utilized the heightened status attributed to *collégiens* as opposed to the technically orientated *apprentis* in the Swiss secondary educational system. Subjects from each group were asked to rate their own group and the out-group on a number of characteristics. Those who rated the in-group, before being told that they would later have to rate the out-group, gave more evaluatively neutral ratings than did subjects who were aware from the beginning that the two sets of ratings would be made. This difference was stronger for *collégiens* than for *apprentis,* and a general conclusion from this experiment was that the higher status *collégiens* rated the in-group more favourably than the out-group, therefore showing in-group bias whereas the reverse was true for the lower status *apprentis.*

A rather different conclusion might be drawn from a study by Branthwaite and Jones (1975) whose subjects were university students in Cardiff who categorized themselves either as English or as Welsh. The experimental procedure was similar to that used by Tajfel *et al.* (1971) and required subjects to allot points to members of the in and out-groups. There was a greater tendency for Welsh subjects to show more discrimination against the English than the reverse. Indeed, English subjects tended to favour the out-group. If one considers that the English have the higher status in terms of political and economic importance, then these results are contrary to those of the Doise and Sinclair study. However, it could be argued that particularly in their capital city the Welsh feel themselves superior. If one could be certain of this, then it might be reasonable to conclude that groups of higher status show greater in-group favouritism.

Such doubts are one of the main problems of studies attempting to adapt real social variables for laboratory experiments. The Turner (1978) experiment manipulated the task-related superiority of one group by instructions, but it seems unclear whether this was relevant to subjects' self-perceptions. In the experiment by Branthwaite and Jones one can form plausible arguments for either group being superior. With such imponderables hanging over crucial variables, it is difficult to form a general conclusion from these studies.

(d) *Inter-group discrimination: conclusions*

Much of the work considered in this chapter in relation to inter-group discrimination has hinged on the work of Tajfel and his collaborators, and it is now appropriate to mention Tajfel's theory of inter-group behaviour (Tajfel, 1978). In addition to being a derivation from and synthesis of past research, Tajfel's theory is intended to be a framework for future investigations, and addresses itself to more large scale problems of social change, rather than solely to experimental work of the type already discussed.

According to the theory, inter-group relations depend on an individual's identification with his group, but it is proposed that this identification is not constant across all occasions. Social situations vary along a continuum from those inducing extremely interpersonal relations, in which individuals react to each other without regard to the groups to which they belong, to those inducing inter-group relations, in which the reverse is the case, individual attributes being irrelevant and only group membership being considered. One consequence of this continuum is an additional continuum of variability versus uniformity in the behaviour towards members of the out-group. At the inter-group extreme members of the in-group will adopt similar behaviour towards all members of the out-group, whereas at the interpersonal extreme, responses being based on individual attributes, behaviour will be correspondingly variable.

Since Tajfel is interested in processes of social change, he discusses a further continuum of social mobility – social change, which refers to an individual's beliefs about the nature of change. At the social mobility end there is an assumption that the social system is adaptable and that an individual may improve his status on the basis of effort or ability. This is contrasted with beliefs at the social change end of the continuum, which encompasses the belief that an individual can only change his status in common with that of his group. It appears that much psychological research which is relevant to changing an individual's status has adopted a belief in social mobility rather than social change (for example, the work of McClelland, Atkinson, Clark and Lowell, 1953 on achievement motivation, and that of Rotter, 1966 on locus of control). Tajfel maintains that it is necessary to understand beliefs at the social change end of the continuum to give a thorough explanation of inter-group discrimination.

A final point of this theory which will be mentioned is the purpose of inter-group relations. It is proposed, in agreement with Turner (1975), that processes of social comparison (Festinger, 1954) are required for an individual to establish his worth on non-objective criteria. Tajfel argues that an individual will only tend to engage in inter-group comparisons when they will result in a positive contribution to his social identity, or, in other words, his self evaluations. There is a tendency to avoid inter-group comparisons which make negative contributions. This point is supported by various empirical data. For example a study by Lemaine (1974) observed groups of children at a summer camp competing against each other. One task was to build a hut, but one of the groups was deprived of some of the necessary materials; this group eventually redefined their task and surrounded their admittedly poorer hut with a garden. It was then necessary to convince the authority that this was a legitimate mode of comparison. It is clearly necessary for a particular dimension to be recognized as valid for comparative purposes, if those, other than in-group members, are to be influenced by it. Nevertheless, this demonstrates how the deprived group avoided a comparison which would have made a negative contribution to members' social identities, and found a dimension (the garden) from which a positive contribution could be made.

While this is only a very brief outline of Tajfel's theory, it is perhaps sufficient to show that it is posing questions that future research may answer, and that the study of inter-group discrimination is by no means confined to the laboratory-based experiments considered earlier. The value of the 'minimal group' studies has already been discussed with respect to Billig's (1976) interpretation of how they demonstrate that social categorization can preserve conditions favouring one group in society over another. This interpretation, together with Tajfel's theory of inter-group behaviour illustrates a relevance of academic social psychology to social problems.

3 Group decision making

One aspect of the social psychology of groups which has received much attention in the last two decades has been the way individuals in a group come to make a joint decision. While some of this attention has been directed to applied fields, such as business negotiations and juries (e.g. Rabbie and Visser, 1972; Nemeth, 1976; McGuire and Bermant, 1977) the work which is to be discussed in this section has been based on an early and apparently remarkable finding that groups tend to make riskier decisions than do the individuals of which they are composed. As such this is an aspect of group psychology which is relevant to the way an individual's attitudes are changed, and is therefore part of cognitive social psychology. It may also be an example of an area of study which has somehow been 'led astray' by the finding from which it developed: the early result, that groups make riskier decisions than individuals (Stoner, 1961) apparently fired the enthusiasm of social psychologists, so that their efforts were directed to explain this 'risky' tendency. It is understandable that this was so, since intuitively one might expect groups, for example in the form of juries or committees, to be more cautious in their decision making. It may have been because of this enthusiasm on the part of social psychologists that they failed to realize that the effect which they were trying to explain was really the result of an experimental artefact.

This section will first discuss this early work, on the phenomenon, which has come to be known as the 'risky shift', and then the explanations offered for it. Following this, the more general topic of 'group polarization' will be considered, since it is this which is the more interesting heir of the risky shift work. Finally, viable explanations of group polarization will be discussed.

(a) *The risky shift*

As already mentioned, the spate of research activity which gave rise to later work on group polarization began with an experiment by Stoner (1961). This was an investigation of the effect of group discussion on individual responses to a set of problems, devised by Wallach and Kogan (1959), to measure risk taking as a personality trait. There were twelve problems, each of which described a central character in a situation in which he had to choose between two courses of action. One of these, the risky course, could, if successful, result in a most desirable outcome, but if unsuccessful it would result in an extremely undesirable one. The cautious course was certain to result in a moderately desirable outcome. Subjects had to imagine they were the central character and select the lowest probability of the risky course being successful which they would require before adopting that course. A selection of a higher probability is thus taken as a more cautious response. Stoner's subjects answered each problem individually, choosing the minimum probability they would require before taking the risky course; they were then formed into groups to discuss each problem and establish a minimum probability which would be acceptable to all group members. He found that the group responses, when averaged over all twelve problems, were significantly lower than the average of the first responses made by the same subjects individually.

This result, then, became the basis of research which followed. It was repeated by Wallach, Kogan and Bem (1962), who again used the Wallach and Kogan (1959) set of problems which came to be known as the Choice Dilemma Questionnaire (CDQ). These authors (Wallach, Kogan and Bem, 1964) suggested that the risky shift could be explained by a diffusion of responsibility. This view held that during the discussion members of the group form affective bonds, so leading to a decrease in the feeling of personal responsibility for the risk. Since there is therefore a feeling of shared responsibility within the group, members are able to accept more risk.

One problem with this interpretation is that the risky shift is attributed to responsibility for the decision, rather than concentrating the explanation on the process of the discussion; and a number of studies in which the discussion was manipulated demonstrated that the diffusion of responsibility explanation was not a viable one. For example, Teger and Pruitt (1967) showed that a group would only shift on items which they had discussed, and argued that if shared responsibility was sufficient to cause shift, then there should be a carry-over effect from discussed to non-discussed items. It was also demonstrated (Lamm, 1967; Ebbeson and Bowers, 1974) that individual shifts could occur after overhearing or watching others' discussions, when it was unlikely that any affective bonds had been formed.

Another early explanation of the risky shift was presented by Brown (1965): the 'cultural value interpretation'. This had two main tenets; first, there is a positive cultural value for risk, so that a moderately risky decision is admired, and second, group discussion serves to make subjects aware of this moderate level of risk which others have decided. The revelation of others' preferences prompts the majority of subjects to shift their decision to the valued extreme. This social comparison mechanism assumes that subjects believe themselves to be closer to the ideal than their fellows. When this misconception is revealed during the discussion, decisions are shifted towards the ideal.

This explanation was supported by studies (e.g. Levinger and Schneider, 1969) which demonstrated that subjects believed their own decisions to be riskier than those which they thought their fellow group members would make. However, their most admired decision was even more risky than their own.

While Brown's cultural value explanation certainly was the most viable of the early interpretations, and led to later ones, an important finding radically altered its focus, and that of research on group decision making. This will now be considered.

(b) *Group polarization and 'choice shifts'*

The important finding influencing this work was reported by Brown (1965) who showed that while the majority of the choice dilemma items shifted to risk, certain items showed consistent shifts to caution. The cultural value explanation was modified, as a result, so as to suggest both a cultural value for risk, and one for caution, depending on the type of decision being made. Brown illustrates this point in the following way: 'Do we praise the father of twelve who scoffs at life insurance and takes mountain climbing for his favourite sport?' (1965, p.705).

The most important lesson to be learnt from the 'cautious shift' finding is a practical one: researchers should not have been so reliant on a single source of decision items, since the CDQ, in the main, produced shifts to risk. It also resulted in a pronounced tendency for explanations to be in terms of risk.

Studies following this finding widened the scope of the area considerably. Moscovici and Zavalloni (1969), and Doise (1969) showed that the risky–cautious dimension was not the only one on which the phenomenon could be demonstrated. They asked subjects to give individual agreement or disagreement to attitude statements and then come to a consensus after group discussion. The group decisions were more extreme than individual agreement or disagreement. An experiment by Myers and Bishop (1970) used the issue of racial attitudes, and showed that group discussion led groups of prejudiced subjects to become more racist in their attitudes, while groups of less prejudiced subjects became more tolerant. Other dimensions on which a similar effect was obtained were as follows: betting behaviour (e.g. Marquis and Reitz, 1969; Blascovich, Ginsberg and Veach, 1975), ethical decisions (e.g. Rettig and Turoff, 1967; Muchlman, Bruker and Ingram, 1976) and person perception (e.g. Andrews and Johnson, 1971; Forgas, 1977).

Returning to the risky–cautious dimension, Fraser, Gouge and Billig (1971) used different (i.e. not CDQ) items and showed that a risky shift resulted when the average of the initial individual decisions was for risk, whereas a cautious shift resulted when the average of the individual preferences was for caution.

Taken together, these studies and others with similar results suggest a general phenomenon: group discussion results in a shift to the extreme nearest to the average of the initial decisions. The phenomenon is now generally termed 'group polarization' (e.g. Myers and Lamm, 1976), although earlier workers (e.g. Pruitt, 1971; Schroeder, 1973) referred to 'choice shifts' to emphasize that it could be demonstrated on many dimensions other than risk.

(c) *Explanations of group polarization*

The generality of the group polarization effect has been amply demonstrated by research, and the evidence necessitates a change of emphasis in the explanations offered for the risky shift. One can scarcely speak of 'diffusion of responsibility for caution'. The cultural value explanation, and its various derivations (e.g. Levinger and Schneider, 1969; Pruitt, 1971) have fared somewhat better and formed two distinct interpretations of group polarization: the social comparison interpretation and the persuasive argument or informational influence interpretation. The main body of research into group polarization in the mid and late 1970s centred round a controversy between these two explanations. These will now be considered, together with two more recent attempts

(Myers and Lamm, 1976; McLachlan, 1979) to integrate them.

The social comparison explanation was basically as proposed by Brown (1965), and has already been outlined. Its salient features are first that one end of the judgmental dimension has normative value, implying that subjects, wanting to perceive and present themselves favourably, will make their decisions nearer to the valued end of the dimension than they believe others will be. Second, when subjects discover that each others' decisions are approximately as valued as their own a shift will occur in the valued direction. They are therefore changing their judgments to maintain a valued image within the group. It is not necessary for subjects to hear each others' reasons for their decisions.

The informational influence explanation (e.g. Burnstein and Vinokur, 1973, 1977) holds that shifts are due to exchange of information which takes place during discussion. It maintains that any subject's decision must be due to those arguments which he has considered, and that in the discussion more will become available, in particular arguments which favour the initially preferred alternative. Thus decisions will be shifted towards the already favoured end of the dimension.

The evidence for the social comparison interpretation falls roughly into two classes. The first examines the relationship between subjects' individual judgments, their expectation of others' judgments and their ideals, and provides substantial evidence that subjects tend to place their own decision between their ideal and their estimate of the average other (e.g. Levinger and Schneider, 1969; Schroeder, 1973). In addition, Jellison and Riskind (1971) showed that extreme judges are admired more by those who are less extreme.

However, less convincing evidence is provided when the relationship is more closely investigated. For example, Myers, Wong and Murdoch (1971) failed to find any relation between a subject's estimate of others' judgment, his own, and his subsequent shift. In addition, there is some evidence (Myers, 1974) that the differences between own, admired and others' judgments are influenced by the order of rating. Burnstein, Vinokur and Pichevin (1974) claimed that extremity of choice is not just a function of value, but of confidence in that choice. Subjects are more confident in their own than in others' decisions, and extreme decisions are admired because they imply a person has reasons for and confidence in that decision.

The second set of studies purporting to provide evidence for the social comparison process examines the effect of interaction limited to the exchange only of subjects' judgments. This form of interaction has been found sufficient to elicit shifts (e.g. Myers, Bach and Schreiber, 1974; Stokes, 1971) although they may be smaller than those elicited by a full discussion (Burnstein, Vinokur and Trope, 1973). These studies contend that the exchange of preferences is a qualitatively different process from that of arguments. However, it is possible to regard exchange of preferences as a limited form of argument exchange. A subject, on learning that the rest of his group are in favour of an extreme decision, is likely to reconsider, or even imagine arguments which he believes may have influenced them. This view explains why a full exchange of arguments produces greater shifts. It also suggests that only those studies in the first set, concerning the difference between own, ideal and others' judgments, adequately assess the social comparison model. It should be remembered, however, that as a group these studies were inconclusive since a number of studies (e.g. Myers, 1974; Myers *et al.*, 1971; and Burnstein *et al.*, 1974) have doubted their conclusions.

Experiments conducted to investigate the informational influence model have typically been more complex in design than those favouring social comparison. It is not possible to test the model adequately by asking subjects to give their reasons for their judgments, but not the specific judgment itself, as the latter may be inferred from their arguments. However, Burnstein and Vinokur (1973) manipulated the type of arguments available by informing subjects that some of the group would be giving arguments in the discussion which favoured their own (i.e. the speaker's) view, while others would be role playing the opposite view by giving arguments supporting the view they did not hold. All subjects in fact gave arguments favouring their own position, although believed that some among their group were role playing the contrary view. The results showed similar shifts as obtained in the control condition in which there was no mention of role playing. Burnstein and Vinokur claim that this implies that subjects shifted as a result of the arguments presented in the discussion, since the social comparison explanation would predict no shift under these conditions, subjects not knowing which pole of the dimension was really valued.

This study was challenged in a replication by Sanders and Baron (1977) who claimed that subjects could make inferences about others' preferences and were able to say whether their fellow group members were telling the truth. Such inferences were thought to act as a basis for comparison which induced a shift. Sanders and Baron in fact concluded that both explanations could contribute to shifts, but this was again denied by Burnstein and Vinokur (1977) who replied that for typical conditions social comparison is neither necessary nor sufficient for group polarization. They claimed that learning that one is in a different initial position from others is only effective in that it makes one rehearse arguments to explain the difference. Arguments still form a crucial part of the explanation.

However, it is difficult to understand why this self-generation of arguments does not lead to arguments for the other side being developed, so resulting in moderation. Also, it seems that any attempt to explain opinion change in terms of arguments, ignoring values or norms, is likely to fail. However, since the social comparison model is not totally in accord with the evidence, one must look to integrations of the two explanations for a satisfactory interpretation.

Such an integration has been provided by Myers and Lamm (1976) who suggest that subjects tend to compare themselves with each other and wish to present themselves favourably relative to others. Such social motivation is said to be able to change attitudes (i.e. cause the polarization phenomenon) through the interpersonal comparison process. In addition, social motivation also leads to the subject expressing socially desirable arguments, so that he makes a verbal commitment of arguments favouring the outer limit of his position. This commitment will also lead to attitude change, in the direction of the arguments expressed. A further important proposition is that this verbal commitment will lead to a rehearsal of arguments for the speaker and a transfer of information for the listener, both of which will lead to increased polarization. In other words, the desire to present and perceive oneself favourably leads to the making of a valued decision. Once this is made a subject feels committed to that view and is concerned to support it overtly with arguments in order to appear consistent with his decision. This overt support, in turn, leads to a more convinced and covert belief in the original decision. At each stage, but particularly the latter, there is a contribution to attitude change and hence to polarization.

The Myers and Lamm theoretical integration uses both the social comparison and the persuasive arguments explanations, and accounts for some of the findings which do not support one or other explanation on its own. For example, it is now explicable why a reduced shift should be found if only decisions and no arguments are exchanged (e.g. Burnstein, Vinokur and Trope, 1973), since in this case neither the verbal commitment nor the increased covert belief in the decision contributes to polarization. Similarly if only arguments, but no decisions are given, there should be a marginally reduced shift.

A more recent explanation of group polarization (McLachlan, 1979) uses the concept of social identity to interpret the shift (see section on inter-group discrimination, earlier in this chapter). McLachlan argues that the social comparison and persuasive argument models rely on normative and informational influence respectively (see Deutsch and Gerard, 1955). Although earlier writers (e.g. Burnstein and Vinokur, 1973) have recognized this, they have not acknowledged that both forms of influence must depend on normative processes since persuasive arguments have value connotations for the group among whom they are exchanged. Thus it is suggested that the arguments put forward in discussion are not objective facts; they are valued statements of opinion. In the experiment, subjects usually adopt a common reference group, based on the population they represent. This group may be defined by the subjects as, for example, 'people who think the same way as me', 'thoughtful students' or even 'competent experimental subjects'. Their interaction in the discussion leads to their affirmation of the values and norms prevalent in that reference group, by the exchange of the individuals' decisions and arguments. Groups will consequently converge and polarize their opinions in the direction of the values which they have affirmed in order to express their social identity.

However, not all experiments on group polarization result in the group converging on a decision, and McLachlan argues that those few in which divergence is found (e.g. Mugny, 1975; Paicheler, 1976) pose problems for the conventional explanations. It is argued that in these studies there were few factors which maintained identification at group level: in one of Mugny's experimental conditions a confederate argued a minority position in a rigid and unyielding fashion resulting in divergence: half the subjects shifted their decisions to the minority and half away from him. Similarly, in Paicheler's experiment some of the groups included a confederate arguing vigorously for the minority position and these groups produced divergence: those subjects holding views near to the confederate's shifted towards her, while those more distant remained steady in their opinion or shifted away from the confederate. In such experiments identification tends to be narrowed to the category defined by the decision under discussion. Subjects may indeed see the issue in terms of intergroup discrimination and diverge their opinions on the only dimension currently available to establish their social identity.

(d) *Group polarization: conclusions*

The group polarization topic presents somewhat of a conflict for social psychologists. In the first place it began with the study of the risky shift which turned out to be more to do with an artefact of experimental materials rather than an interesting social phenomenon. Secondly, as pointed out by Eiser (1980), the group discussion is a somewhat artificial situation. Finally, it has produced such an enormous amount of research that one is left wondering what was so special about group polarization that caught the imagination of social psychologists, when other topics more obviously relevant to social problems did not. There is little evidence that a real group makes decisions in the way social psychologists propose their subjects do in these experiments, but then real decisions are rarely open to this sort of investigation as they are seldom made on rating scales. So what is the point of all these studies?

Myers and Lamm (1976) suggest that group polarization is a relevant social phenomenon if one sees it in a wider context than the experimental discussion group studied. They consider that it is a type of attitude change which is applied by a group of people to an individual. Most of the conventional studies of attitude change (see Chapter 2) tell us how one persuasive communicator can influence a number of people, but in the group polarization paradigm the numbers are reversed – several people are influencing one. This paradigm is relevant therefore if one is interested in, for example, how an individual's knowledge of the latest opinion poll can influence his attitude, or how a reference group can influence one of its members. It appears that a group, by stating its values and beliefs, can cause its members to change their attitudes in the direction advocated. Similarly, an opinion poll will presumably influence individuals' beliefs in the direction of the majority view. Whether this happens through a process of social comparison, informational influence, social identity, or some mixture of the two former mechanisms is open to debate. However, in view of topics discussed earlier in the book one cannot be surprised that it does happen.

4 Conclusions: group influences on judgmental decisions

All the topics discussed in this chapter have been concerned with the way a group can influence how individuals make decisions. The decisions themselves are not particularly important, and are of the kind that have been investigated in earlier chapters. For example attitudinal judgment involves a decision, perhaps with a commitment to a particular point on some dimension. In this chapter the focus has so far been on how a group can affect the way that decision is made or changed.

Previous chapters have emphasized how the particular topics they dealt with could be considered, with advantage, under the notion of consistency. This has not been stressed in this chapter, not because it is irrelevant, but because the focus has been elsewhere. It is now important to consider how group influences on decision making are in many cases mediated by consistency.

In Chapter 1 consistency was seen as a characteristic of cognitions about social events and as having particular functions. One of these is to allow the world to be a predictable place to its perceivers; another related function is to allow the individual to construct reality so as to enhance his self-esteem. The areas of group influence discussed in this chapter demonstrate both functions. Group polarization has been seen as explicable in terms of social comparison processes, which entail, in essence, an attempt to be more valued on a value dimension than one's fellow subjects. Surely this is an endeavour to increase self-esteem. If group polarization is explained by the persuasive arguments model then judgments are presumably being made more consistent with information as it becomes available in the discussion. Not to shift one's judgment in accordance with relevant information would be a curious and inconsistent response.

The more recent explanation in terms of social identity is similar to many of the phenomena considered in the section on inter-group discrimination. As outlined by Turner (1975) social identity is an attempt to maximize positive self-esteem. In some of the experiments discussed subjects tend to be in peculiar and probably incomprehensible situations, and to establish positive social identity, or self-esteem in these situations, they compare themselves favourably with others on the only dimension the experiment allows. Whether this dimension is in terms of points being allotted to different groups, as in the 'minimal group' experiments, or in terms of a decision dimension like risk–caution as in group polarization is immaterial. Subjects still seem to want to ensure that in an incomprehensible situation they have positive self-esteem. Perhaps this is an adaptive response as it at least allows the possibility of being able to cope with the unknown, and maybe to imagine that it will be a consistent and therefore predictable unknown.

6 When consistency fails

Throughout the previous four chapters we have seen that cognitive social psychologists use the notion of consistency to explain many aspects of their discipline. It has also been seen that those theories which do not invoke consistency as an explanatory mechanism, of, for example, attitudes (e.g. Sherif and Hovland, 1961), or attraction (e.g. Byrne, 1961a; Thibaut and Kelley, 1959), sometimes appear to be less satisfactory as theories of cognitive social behaviour. This chapter will briefly reconsider the functions of consistency in social behaviour, and then discuss what may happen when the principles these functions use are no longer applicable, or are, for some reason, abandoned.

I Functions of consistency

The first chapter discussed the functions of consistency, suggesting that we assume that others' behaviour, attitudes and attributes will be consistent, probably to a greater extent than they actually are; in doing so we are able to make a prediction about their behaviour or attributes based on some other knowledge of that person. If you know, for example, that your great aunt enjoys toffees and has little regard for her dental hygiene, you may predict that she will have few natural teeth. You may be wrong, but the possibility of being wrong is the price one pays for relying on any rule-of-thumb prediction. It is more likely that you are correct, and you can decide upon the advisability of offering her crunchy biscuits or raw carrots, or even of suggesting a trip to the dentist.

This assumption of consistency, then, allows us to predict other people's behaviour and attitudes, and without it social life would seem incoherent and confused. It can be no exaggeration to say that social life is dependent upon social behaviour being predictable. Since man is essentially social, requiring others' company throughout his life, it is important that he is able to predict and explain, at least some of the time, how those others will react; hence the widespread use of consistency to interpret and guide social behaviour.

Although we expect social behaviour to be reasonably predictable, this itself is dependent upon an assumption not yet mentioned. We can only predict another's behaviour if that person aims to avoid misunderstandings. If your aunt, for whatever reason, merely pretends to enjoy toffees, but instead of eating them slips them into the front of her dress, then she will be engaging in some role-playing activity, and your attempts to predict her later behaviour, based on consistency, may well fail. Besides role-playing, a more widespread behaviour in which there is no aim to avoid misunderstandings is humour. As we shall see a number of humour theorists (e.g. Koestler, 1964; McGhee, 1979) have relied on the principle of inconsistency, or incongruity, to explain humour.

A further important function of consistency as discussed in Chapter 1 is in its relationship to value. We value other people who are consistent, presumably because they are predictable and make life easy for us. Similarly, consistency is linked to positive self-esteem; to a certain extent we value our own behaviour when it is consistent. In most conditions consistency is a favourable attribute, one which we endeavour to maintain, and therefore when we are consistent, we support our self-esteem. In some instances this may be done by describing ourselves or our opinions in positively valued terms, and in doing so making a more consistent description (Eiser and Mower White, 1974a, 1975; see Chapter 2). In others we do it by attempting to establish positive social identity (Turner, 1975) by comparing ourselves favourably with others on the most appropriate (or in some cases the only) dimension the situation allows.

The relationship between consistency and positive self-esteem has also been emphasized by various theorists concerned with psychopathology (e.g. Rogers, 1959), but in the reverse direction. That is, low self-esteem or lack of self acceptance leads to inconsistent behaviour. Although it might be critical in a clinical setting, the direction of causality between self-esteem and consistency is for the present discussion immaterial. It is sufficient to emphasize that the two are crucially linked and may well reinforce each other.

2 What happens when consistency is abandoned?

(a) *When social behaviour is not predictable*

It may be argued that the picture drawn of social behaviour in terms of consistency is particularly banal and boring. One might suggest that there are many instances in which people go out of their way to be unpredictable, and of course this is true. Entertainers and humorists for example, whether professional or amateur, are often engaged in unpredictable and inconsistent behaviour. We also know certain people who delight in being unpredictable, who like to show they are different from others. Although this behaviour certainly exists, can be explained, and in the latter case is probably an instance of being predictable on dimensions different from that on which others may be predicted, it is relatively rare. Much of social life *is* predictable and banal. Nevertheless we do occasionally find instances of entertainment or humour; these cannot be fitted into the predictable and consistent picture of social behaviour. Some attempt will be made to consider them in this section.

Little has been written about the psychology of entertainment or literature, apart from that of humour which will be discussed later. Probably the most preferred explanation for literature has been of a psychoanalytic nature, Freud's (1900) interpretation of the myth of Oedipus being an obvious example. Similarly Bettelheim (1978) has interpreted traditional fairy stories as being the way in which a child can work through his fantasies and achieve an understanding of his conscious self in a reassuring manner. A rather different, but non-contradictory, explanation could be offered in terms of consistency. Much literature is inconsistent with our expectations of the world, and it is often this inconsistency which gives it appeal. This can be seen at both simple and sophisticated levels. For example, the children's story of 'The Three Little Pigs' (see, e.g. Briggs, 1970) would scarcely be of interest if the wolf, having eaten the first two little pigs, also ate the third. This ending would accord with the expectations that the initial part of the story had induced, and would be consistent with reality (if one assumes that wolves do eat pigs living in houses). However, a consistent ending such as this would make a dull and unappealing story.

Adults' literature, in contrast to children's, often makes use of inconsistencies within a particular character's personality, perhaps portraying him as a complex and therefore interesting individual. Psychologists may not yet be in a position to say whether such a picture mirrors reality (see Hampson, 1982). However it may be that the inconsistencies and complexities drawn within such a picture are at odds with our expectations of reality, which, as discussed in Chapter 1, are probably more simple and consistent than is reality itself. The inconsistencies between our expectations of a simple character, and the more complex one drawn by an author often provide the attraction of literature. For example, Shakespeare's Othello, an apparently devoted husband and wise ruler, becomes so racked with jealousy over what he assumes is his wife's (albeit rather trivial) behaviour that he kills her and then himself, on discovering his mistake. Presumably, in a consistent story, he would have accepted the explanation of her behaviour, and the tragedy would have been averted, but Shakespeare would have had no story to tell.

Theories of humour

The last decade has seen an enormous increase in research on humour and a particular concentration on children's humour – its characteristics and the way in which it develops with age. This section will be mainly concerned with this recent trend rather than with early philosophical or non experimental works on humour (e.g. Beattie, 1776; Hobbes, 1651; McDougall, 1903; Spencer, 1860). For a discussion of such theories the reader should refer to Keith-Spiegel (1972).

Perhaps two initial points should be made with regard to a discussion about humour. The first is that humour does have a place in a book about social psychology, even though this book is unusual in this respect. One can justify this in a number of ways: conventionally, one does not laugh at one's own jokes, but at other people's. Freud (1905) argued that jokes are necessarily a social phenomenon because not only are they for others, but that others appreciating a joke must share the joker's inhibitions: in Freudian theory jokes represent acceptable forms of unconscious and repressed desires, and release these unacceptable desires into consciousness, in a somewhat similar way to the release by dreaming. Pleasure is gained by a saving of psychic energy otherwise used in the repression. For a joke to be appreciated, it is therefore necessary for joker and listener to share similar repressions. A further reason may be that jokes are often about social issues or entities (for example ethnic groups), and it is not hard to imagine that a person's attitude towards an ethnic group may be involved in his appreciation of such humour.

The second point is that many theories of humour have used inconsistency as an explanatory mechanism, but that it has tended to be termed 'incongruity'. The latter term will be used in this section, on the understanding that it is interchangeable with 'inconsistency' as used in the rest of the book.

This section will first consider the so-called 'Incongruity theories' (e.g. Keith-Spiegel, 1972, p.7) and the more recent developments (e.g. McGhee, 1979) of the theories which use incongruity as an explanatory mechanism. It is these which, in the main, are responsible for the upsurge of developmental theories of humour, possibly because children's humour has been viewed in relation to a child's growing cognitive abilities rather than the other changes, and cognitive aspects of humour have been the concern of the incongruity theorists. Second, there will be a discussion of non-incongruity theories of humour, together with the suggestions (e.g. Rothbart, 1977; Suls, 1977) that many such explanations are best encompassed by the notion of incongruity.

(i) *Incongruity and developmental theories of humour*
McGhee, perhaps the most influential of recent writers about humour has suggested that incongruity is a necessary but insufficient prerequisite for humour. In this sense, incongruity refers to 'absurd, unexpected, inappropriate, and otherwise out-of-context events' (1979, p.42). The way the incongruity is processed will determine whether it is perceived as humorous – it may for example arouse only curiosity or anxiety. McGhee, and indeed other incongruity theorists, are therefore concerned with the cognitive aspects of humour, rather than with physiological, psychodynamic or behavioural aspects. While some of these other aspects are discussed among the non-incongruity theories, McGhee proposes that they are either by-products or modifiers of humour and are therefore secondary to incongruity. This may be the key to the success of the incongruity theories.

One model in this group, from which later theories have developed, is that of Suls (1972), who proposed a two stage information processing routine which describes humour as a problem solving activity. Suls suggested that perception of the incongruity is the first stage in the process but that for humour to be experienced the incongruity must be resolved. In the first stage the joke contradicts experience, thus providing incongruity, and in the second stage information is retrieved from whatever source (the joke or previous experience) which will explain the incongruity.

This two stage model has a fair amount of empirical support. Shultz (1972), for example, demonstrated that seven and eleven year old children found both incongruity and its resolution important for humour appreciation. Subjects were presented with original cartoons, and with those from which the incongruity or the resolution had been removed, and showed a tendency first to identify the incongruity and then to resolve it. In cartoons in which one or other aspect had been removed, subjects typically invented the missing element. A later study (Shultz, 1974a) indicated that the information given in verbal jokes is processed in the order predicted by the two stage model: that is, the incongruity was first perceived, and the resolution information was not detected until it was required to resolve the incongruity. For cartoons, however, the order was more varied.

Furthermore, Shultz (1976) argues that the two-stage process in humour appreciation does not develop until about seven years, and coincides with the onset of concrete operational thought (Piaget, 1952). Before this period, during preoperational thought, unresolved incongruities are found to be humorous.

Suls's model and the evidence provided by Shultz have not gone unquestioned by humour theorists. Rothbart (1977) and Rothbart and Pien (1977) point out that some jokes provide resolution but in doing so introduce an additional incongruity. An example provided by Rothbart and Pien (p.37) is as follows:

> 'Why did the elephant sit on the marshmallow?
> Because he didn't want to fall into the hot chocolate.'

The initial incongruity, an elephant on a marshmallow, is to some extent resolved, but one is left with a new element of incongruity – that of an elephant sitting in a cup of hot chocolate. According to Rothbart (1976) incongruity is sufficient to elicit humour provided that it is perceived in a joking or playful context and this is so for adults and children alike. In addition, Pien and Rothbart (1980) propose that infants of about four months of age are capable of appreciating incongruity humour, since they are capable of detecting incongruities and also of playful assimilation (i.e. assimilation without serious accommodation) (Piaget, 1962).

Another incongruity theory has been proposed by Nerhardt (1976, 1977). This suggests that humour is a consequence of 'the discrepancy between two mental representations, one of which is an expectation and the other is some other idea or a percept' (1977, p.47). While this basic proposition is similar to other incongruity theories, Nerhardt's work does suggest some differences from other theorists. Firstly, humour is said to increase as the discrepancy increases and his theory provides a method of determining discrepancy in terms of mental classes. He also maintains that incongruity defined in this way will be a personal variable, and that one must be cautious when treating it objectively. While one might think it necessarily the case that discrepancies between objects of perception and expectations about them are different for different individuals, since presumably their expectations vary, this phenomenological approach is novel in the study of humour. Furthermore it is not readily able to be incorporated into the theories of Suls, Rothbart or McGhee.

A further difference in Nerhardt's work is that the stimulus material he uses to gain his evidence is not obviously or recognizably humorous. For example, in one study (1970) subjects were asked to lift weights. If a container of certain weight is repeatedly lifted, lifting a container of very different weight appears to be humorous. A further study, quoted in support of Nerhardt's theory, is that of Shurcliff (1968). In this experiment students were asked to perform a task; in one condition they were asked to handle a docile rat in an experimental situation, in another they were asked to take a small amount of blood from a rat, and in a final condition they were asked to take a large amount of blood from an aggressive rat. Following these instructions, at the start of the task, the rat was found to be a toy and subjects were asked to rate the humour, anxiety and suprisingness of the situation. While Shurcliff found a significant positive trend between increasing humour and both anxiety and surprisingness, and himself interpreted the results according to arousal theory (Berlyne, 1960), Nerhardt suggests that they may be seen as exemplifying how increasing divergence from expectations (the task instructions) results in increasing humour.

The final theorist whose work will be discussed in this section is McGhee (1974, 1977, 1979, 1980). Throughout his work there is an emphasis on the view that incongruity is the only necessary condition for humour and that it comes closest to being its foundation stone. Another position which McGhee takes is that humour can only occur with a playful mood or attitude, a view supported by Rothbart (e.g. 1976) but not by Nerhardt. McGhee interprets humour as a cognitive event and claims that it develops in children with their other cognitive abilities. Jokes and cartoons are seen as problems to be solved, and humour is an intellectual challenge, with problems or jokes in the middle range of difficulty being most appreciated. A joke which is too obvious is no challenge, whereas one which is too difficult is too much like hard work. In support of this McGhee (1972, 1974) describes the 'Fat Ethel Joke', demonstrating that the intended humour should not be understood until a child has acquired concrete operational thought and understands the principle of conservation of quantity.

> Fat Ethel sat down at the lunch counter and ordered a whole fruit cake.
> 'Shall I cut it into four or eight pieces?' asked the waitress.
> 'Four', said Ethel, 'I'm on a diet.'

It should also be pointed out that adult readers should not find Fat Ethel's behaviour particularly funny, because it is presumably some years since they attained conservation of quantity, and therefore the joke does not represent much intellectual challenge.

McGhee (1979) proposes a theory of humour development in four stages in accordance with a child's increasing cognitive ability. Stage 1 begins early in the second year when a child is able to represent objects with internal images and can therefore make a pretend action with an object in its absence, or in the presence of an inappropriate action. It is notable that McGhee's proposal for the first instance of humour is considerably later than that of Pien and Rothbart (1980) who argue that four-month-old infants have the capacity for play and are able to detect incongruity, and can therefore experience humour. McGhee and Chapman (1980) argue against this view, claiming that playfulness and the perception of incongruity may not be sufficient to ensure humour, and that the evidence on which Pien and Rothbart base their view (studies by Sroufe and Waters, 1976; and Sroufe and Wunsch, 1972) is insufficient to support their position.

McGhee's stage 2 begins at the end of the second year and

is shown by a child giving incongruous labels to objects: dogs may be called 'cats' or eyes 'ears'. Stage 3 is one of conceptual incongruities: a three-year-old finds it humorous to imagine, for instance, a cat with a variety of uncatlike characteristics. A child at stage 4 is beginning to have a similar form of humour as that of adults, which often relies on words having multiple meanings. This stage begins at about seven years, and is characterized by an enjoyment of riddles.

This last stage has been the subject of more detailed investigation: humour appears to rely on the ambiguity of words, and riddles are the central attraction up to about ten years of age (Sutton-Smith, 1975). Shultz (1974b) and Shultz and Horibe (1974) have made a detailed study of the development of linguistic ambiguity at this age, demonstrating that the first form to be appreciated is phonological ambiguity. Shultz and Horibe give the following examples:

> 'Waiter, what's this?'
> 'That's bean soup, ma'am.'
> 'I'm not interested in what it's been, I'm asking what it is now' (p.14).

Lexical ambiguities are appreciated soon after:

> 'Order! Order in the court!'
> 'Ham and cheese on rye, please, Your Honour' (p.14).

At about eleven or twelve years old jokes based on deep and surface structure ambiguity are understood:

> 'Tell me how long cows should be milked.'
> 'They should be milked the same as short ones, of course.' (surface structure ambiguity)
>
> 'What animal can jump as high as a tree?'
> 'All animals – trees cannot jump.
> (deep structure ambiguity)
> (Shultz, 1974b, p.101)

The final developmental aspect of humour to be considered is McGhee's (1980) longitudinal study of the way in which children may develop a sense of humour. The latter term is used to describe individual differences in both initiation and appreciation of humour. It is a particularly ambitious and successful study concerning the antecedents of humour (chiefly early mothering and child behaviour). Information about maternal behaviour was available from birth onwards, and that about the child's behaviour from age three to eleven, in some cases, and both were collected before the study was instigated. Humour data was collected while the children were at nursery school or day camp. McGhee demonstrated that maternal behaviour appeared less important than a child's own early behaviour in predicting a later sense of humour. It seems that children with a heightened sense of humour are dominant and aggressive towards their peers both before and after starting school. In addition, these children had precocious language development, and for preschool children, greater height and weight. It was suggested that these characteristics might aid dominance behaviour, and verbal and physical aggressiveness. In terms of maternal behaviour, mothers who are protective and generally approving, but not affectionate appear to produce children with an increased sense of humour; McGhee suggests that the link here could be that lack of affection may lead to a child being aggressive.

He further proposes that humour provides a socially acceptable behaviour for channelling aggressive impulses, and indeed may well be a behaviour which is positively reinforced by adults. Further, by initiating humour, a child (or adult) can dominate a conversation, and this accords with the aggressive, dominant, talkative child who develops into a humorist. An additional cluster of behaviours which predicted later humour was related to receiving favourable reactions from adults. This may be concerned both with humour being an ideal means of getting such reactions, and to the same children being aggressive and dominating towards their peers: such behaviour may make them unpopular, giving a subsequent need for adult approval.

This study should provide an ideal starting point for future experimental work since many of the links between maternal and early behaviours and humour remain unexplored. It does however suffer from the normal problems of a longitudinal study as McGhee and Chapman (1980) point out. Specific difficulties are that since the oldest subjects were only eleven years McGhee cannot make predictions beyond that age, and that no data are available for fathers, who may in fact be the most important models for humour, particularly as humour initiation is more characteristic of men. Nevertheless, McGhee's study is the first and so far only one to make use of longitudinal methods; it organizes a large quantity of data, and provides some intriguing suggestions as to the origins of humour development.

(ii) *Incongruity and developmental theories of humour: a conclusion*

The last section considered incongruity theories together with the way in which humour develops in children, even though the two may at first sight not be obvious companions. The reasons should now be apparent: first, the same theorists have been involved in both aspects, and second, in formulating notions about incongruity humour, psychologists have necessarily had to consider cognitive mechanisms, and abilities. The most apparent source of differing cognitive abilities is in the development of the child's intellectual capacities. Hence incongruity theorists' reliance on the development of humour and, in particular, on its relation to Piagetian stages of intellectual development. However, not all work in this field is related only to intellectual development. McGhee's longitudinal study on the development of a sense of humour places more emphasis on interaction with peers and adults.

In contrast to the following section on non-incongruity theories of humour, the incongruity theories present a united front, their main tenet being, obviously, that incongruity is a necessary condition for humour. Different theories pay more or less attention to various aspects of humour. Nerhardt, for example, is not concerned with its development, but is in a sense more sophisticated than the others in that he utilizes a measure of incongruity. Other points on which incongruity theorists differ are the earliest age at which humour may begin, whether a playful attitude is an essential condition, and whether the incongruity must necessarily be resolved. It may be that there are no definitive answers to these questions, a possible conclusion being that differing conceptions of humour, or different ages of children enjoying it may lead to different views on each question. Nevertheless, it appears that in spite of these problems raised by incongruity humour, the theories have provided the most detailed analyses and data of all psychological theories of humour.

(iii) *Non-incongruity theories of humour*

Of necessity this section must be concerned with a number of theories which have little in common with each other. In contrast to the previous section describing incongruity theories which are all concerned with the cognitive characteristics of humour, those discussed in this section are concerned with a variety of aspects of humour. For example, social, motivational and physiological aspects are considered and it is not surprising, therefore, that these theories are relatively varied. As will be seen, however, they may be broadly divided into those concerned with function, and those interested in the way jokes are constructed.

Freud's theory of humour Freud's (1905, 1928) psychoanalytic views on humour are among the earliest which will be considered in this section. He believed humour to be the result of repressed sexual and aggressive wishes, which have been forced into the unconscious due to society's prohibition of their expression. Jokes, however, are not prohibited, and indeed in some cases are socially valued, and they thus provide an acceptable outlet for repressed wishes. The sexual or aggressive nature of humour is often disguised, and may not be recognized unless the recipient shares the same repressions as the joker. Repression involves the use of psychic energy, which will be saved when the joke is made and repression is no longer necessary. This saving of energy is demonstrated, according to Freud, by our pleasure in and laughter at the humour.

Even this brief summary of Freud's work on humour must indicate that he was less concerned with a description of humour than with what humour is for. Its function, according to Freudian views, is to regulate sexual and aggressive wishes. Function is an aspect not considered by incongruity theories, who are concerned with a description of cognitive characteristics. Another component of Freud's work however, bears more resemblance to that of the incongruity theorists. Freud refers to the technique of making jokes, or the way a joke is constructed, as 'joke-work', and describes a number of techniques, most of which refer to trivial or non-tendentious jokes: condensation, displacement, absurdity, faulty reasoning, representation by the opposite and analogy. Condensation, which Freud (1905) recognizes as 'the core of the technique of verbal jokes' (p.88) involves a kind of abbreviation and economy of expression. Puns are one example of this technique, multiple uses of the same material are others. However, it could be argued that such jokes may rely on incongruity in that the different uses of the same material seldom anticipate similar expectations.

Nevertheless, the construction of jokes is a relatively minor point and is made in Freud's work to emphasize how the mechanisms of joke-work resemble dream-work. As Kline (1977) points out, jokes and dreams have a similar function in Freudian theory: to allow acceptable expression of aggressive and sexual desires. In this way, Freud incorporated his views on humour into his main work on psychoanalytic theory. Kline (1972) regards it as an unimportant part from the viewpoint of the theory. This is undoubtedly so in that the ideas on humour could be refuted while leaving the rest of Freudian theory intact. Nevertheless, relatively recently developed aspects of psychoanalytic therapy have used humour and jokes, often as mechanisms for elucidating a patient's repressions (e.g. Grossman, 1977; Levine, 1977; Mindess, 1976; O'Connell, 1976, 1977) even though Kubie (1971) has expressed the view that humour is detrimental to the therapeutic process. It is thus perhaps too early to be certain that the theory of humour is an unimportant aspect of Freud's work.

A question which is sometimes considered, with regard to Freud's work is whether his theories are accurate representations of reality. In this instance, is this really what jokes are for? Philosophers (e.g. Popper, 1959) have taken the view that a theory is only as good as the testable hypotheses it can generate, and psychologists have often followed this view, considering that only theories leading to experimentally verifiable hypotheses are scientific and therefore worthy of their discipline. This view poses a problem for psychologists who would like to believe that Freud was the most influential founder of their discipline, since it can be readily shown (e.g. Eysenck and Wilson, 1973) that psychoanalytic theory is rarely amenable to scientific investigation. There seem to be two solutions to this dilemma: the first, advocated by Eysenck and Wilson, is to argue that since Freudian theory is unscientific it should be abandoned in favour of more rigorous lines of thought. The second solution, and the conclusion adopted here, admits that Freud's views cannot be contained within a totally scientific psychology, but that to eliminate them from consideration and enquiry would exclude the greatest wealth of ideas that psychology possesses. Freudian theory is not concerned with being experimentally verifiable, as Freud (e.g. 1900, 1933) himself admitted. It is concerned with providing ideas and speculations and giving insights into human behaviour without which psychology would be immeasurably poorer.

Having reached this conclusion, it needs to be said that certain writers (e.g. Kline, 1977) believe that they have been able to form hypotheses from Freud's work on humour, and Kline (1972) discusses some of the experimental studies resulting from such hypotheses. In view of the conclusion above, it is not proposed to consider these here, but interested readers should refer to Kline (1972) and to the Eysenck and Wilson (1973) review of his work.

Social interaction functions of humour A number of psychologists have, like Freud, concentrated their efforts in the field of humour, on the function rather than the construction of jokes. Fairly obviously for social psychologists, social interaction is seen as an important function. It appears that much of the work which falls into this category is based on observation and speculation rather than experiment, but is far less detailed and insightful than Freud's contributions.

It will be seen whether this work has been helpful in understanding humour.

An early contribution, provided by Radcliffe-Brown (1940), suggests that people often find themselves in close interpersonal relationships with others who are not of their choice. In such a situation, for example an in-law relationship, it is important to diffuse any antagonism which may occur. A joking relationship combining friendship and conflict may suffice and is a common occurrence in a number of cultures. This view is similar to Freud's suggestion that humour functions as an acceptable expression of aggressive and sexual wishes.

A more detailed analysis has been provided by Martineau (1972) who proposes that humour can be used to initiate and facilitate communication and that it fosters the development of social relationships. This model outlines the functions of humour initiated in intra-group and inter-group situations, and claims that such functions depend upon how the humour is perceived by members of each group. For example in an intra-group situation if humour is judged to esteem the group it will solidify the group; if it is judged to disparage the ingroup then it may control ingroup behaviour. For example, jokes about being late for a meeting have this function of reinforcing violated norms of the group. However, similar judgments about inter-group humour can, according to Martineau, control or solidify the ingroup or foster conflict within, or demoralization and disintegration of the group. Similarly, humour in an inter-group situation can affect ingroup and outgroup members, depending upon by whom it is initiated and upon how it is perceived by whom. Martineau lists and finds functions for all possible permutations of these variables, but he provides little indication of which function will be adopted other than can be found in the particular joke in question. For example, humour initiated by an outgroup member and perceived by the ingroup as disparaging the ingroup may either (a) increase morale and solidify the ingroup (b) control the behaviour of the ingroup, or (c) foster demoralization and disintegration of the ingroup. The problem with this model, it seems, is that there is no indication which of these radically different possibilities will occur. Furthermore, to make such a distinction one suspects it would be necessary to have information about the joke and the participants in the situation, when the particular function of the humour might appear obvious. It is scarcely surprising that this model, providing all but the essential information to determine the obvious, has not advanced the psychology of humour very far.

Kane, Suls and Tedeschi (1977) criticize Martineau in that he does not explain why humour should be used in the various inter-group situations when praise or criticism might be equally functional. Their work interprets humour as having the function of social influence, through its essential quality of ambiguity. Humorous communications can be interpreted in a variety of ways allowing for a retraction of the communication if the recipient reacts unfavourably. The functions they consider include self disclosure; a person may wish to communicate an intention or value so as to allow himself to disclaim the intention if he receives an unfavourable reaction. Further, he can use humour in a decommitment function so as to deny any harmful intention and dissociate himself from the responsibility of earlier behaviour. Kane *et al.* suggest also that humour may be used as a face-saving device to preserve self-esteem after an embarrassing incident (see e.g. Edelmann and Hampson, 1979); as an unmasking tactic to reveal hypocrisy and pretentions of others; as an antecedent of interpersonal attraction; and as a safe method of ingratiation of powerful others. For all these functions Kane *et al.* provide anecdotal examples, and empirical evidence, where it exists, to demonstrate that the ambiguity surrounding humour can be used to advantage by shifting its perceived meaning according to situational factors.

It appears that the work of Kane *et al.* is amongst the more useful in elucidating the functions of humour in social interactions. Although it is not based entirely on empirical evidence, it provides a scheme from which testable hypotheses can be derived, in contrast to Martineau's model, which merely lists possible functions of humour in a variety of intra- and inter-group situations. Nevertheless none of the investigations of the interactional functions of humour can be claimed as major advances, possibly because social psychologists seem to have concentrated their efforts on laughter rather than on humour (e.g. Chapman, 1973, 1975; Foot and Chapman, 1976; Giles and Oxford, 1970). It follows, therefore, that the field of social functions of humour as opposed to laughter, is relatively unexplored.

Berlyne's arousal theory of humour Berlyne's (1969a, 1972) views on humour are to a great extent an offshoot of his more general arousal theory (e.g. 1960, 1967, 1969b). The latter holds that arousal, described as an 'intervening variable' (1967, p.12) and determined by various physiological indices, has a close relationship with both pleasure, as shown through verbal reports, and reinforcement. An early version (1960) of arousal theory held that an increase in arousal to 'uncomfortable levels' (1972, p.46) may be reinforcing if it is quickly followed by a larger decrease, although the necessary time span was not specified. This so-called 'arousal-jag' concept was retracted (Berlyne, 1967) on the basis of physiological evidence (e.g. Meyers, Valenstein and Lacy, 1963; Soltysik, 1960; Yoshi and Tsukiyama, 1952), and replaced by the 'arousal-boost'. The latter suggests that a moderate rise in arousal is associated with pleasure or reward.

Berlyne (1972) suggests that both arousal-boosts and arousal-jags may join to contribute to the pleasurable experience of humour in a mechanism he terms an 'arousal boost-jag' (p.46). In this case, it is claimed, the rise in arousal caused by the joke is sufficiently moderate to be within the scope of the arousal-boost mechanism, but a subsequent drop in arousal may increase the enjoyment by the arousal reduction mechanism.

In support of these views, Berlyne cites evidence provided by Zigler, Levine and Gould (1967) that moderately difficult cartoons were most appreciated by children aged 8-13 years, suggesting that the arousal-jag is responsible. The initial challenge and incomprehension of the joke or cartoon presumably raises arousal to uncomfortable levels, while resolution reduces it. This may be some kind of physiological explanation for the phenomenon described by McGhee (1972, 1974) and discussed earlier. Children are most appreciative of humour which demonstrates their most recently acquired cognitive skills, jokes in the middle range of difficulty being the most challenging and enjoyable. A joke which is too simple is no challenge and does not allow arousal to rise into the uncomfortable range. One which is too difficult is too demanding for existing cognitive abilities, and presumably does not allow arousal to fall after its initial rise to an uncomfortable level.

While Berlyne's views may give an alternative and plausible explanation of this particular aspect of the development of humour, they pose numerous problems, and, in addition, can be incorporated into an incongruity framework. The major problem with Berlyne's general arousal theory (and with the views of other arousal theorists; e.g. Fiske and Maddi, 1961; Schultz, 1965; Zuckerman, 1969) is that the physiological basis of the concept of arousal is not described clearly enough (Inglis, 1975), and that the use of the concept can be covered by existing terms such as drive state or adaptation level (Andrew, 1974). There is little sense then in using a blanket term with imprecise meaning whether in general psychology or in theories of humour.

Rothbart (1973) has argued that arousal increases of any size are accompanied by an experience of pleasure when the subject judges that the situation is non-threatening. While this in no way solves the problem of the imprecise meaning of the term, it does explain various physiological data and allow her (Rothbart, 1977) to adapt arousal theory to an incongruity theory of humour.

Godkewitsch (1976) measured heart rate and skin conductance both during the initial part of the joke and the punch line. According to Berlyne's arousal-jag mechanism arousal should rise during the initial part and fall on hearing the punch line. This however was not the case; as judged by these particular physiological measures, arousal was increased by the punch line. In addition, ratings of the joke's funniness were positively related to arousal induced by the punch line. Rothbart (1977) argues that this supports her position that any increase in arousal is pleasurable if perceived in a non-threatening situation.

In addition, Rothbart (1976) proposes that, in an incongruity theory framework, it is not necessary for the incongruity to be resolved in order that humour is experienced. As discussed earlier, incongruity theorists disagree as to whether this is so, Shultz (1976) and Suls (1972) proposing that humour will only follow the resolution of an incongruity. Following her position, Rothbart (1977) argues that arousal and incongruity theories are not incompatible but merely represent analyses of humour at different levels of abstraction. Incongruity can lead to an increase in arousal, which according to Rothbart, is pleasurable if it is a joking or non-threatening situation. There is no requirement for resolution or decrease in arousal for the experience of humour, since neither is necessitated by Rothbart's work.

The argument that arousal and incongruity are compatible explanations of humour at different levels of abstraction has undoubted force. Nevertheless, it must be remembered that as a general explanatory concept in psychology arousal has been questioned (e.g. Andrew, 1974) and one doubts, therefore, whether the physiological level of explanation it offers for humour has much validity. It certainly cannot challenge the incongruity theories.

Superiority theories of humour While Freud and certain social psychologists are interested in the functions of humour, other theorists, like Berlyne and those advocating an incongruity approach are concerned with the way jokes are constructed and analysed. In this latter group may be included a number of theorists who propose the 'disparagement theories' (Suls, 1977, p.41). These have been variously called 'superiority theory' (e.g. Keith-Spiegel, 1972; La Fave, Haddad and Maesen, 1976), or 'disposition theory' (e.g. Zillmann and Cantor, 1976) and are based on the idea that humour results from observation of other people's infirmities, particularly when we compare ourselves favourably with those others. Perhaps one of the earlier writers to describe this aspect of humour was Hobbes (1651) who proposed that laughter is caused by 'the apprehension of some deformed thing in another, by comparison whereof they suddenly applaud themselves' (1968, p.125). Other than moralizing on the shortcomings of this aspect of human behaviour, Hobbes says little more about humour. Nevertheless, other more recent writers have followed his view and elaborated superiority theories.

One of the more explicit statements of superiority theory comes from Zillmann and Cantor (1976) whose 'disposition model' includes the use of a continuum of affective disposition from extremely positive to extremely negative. They claim that humour appreciation varies inversely with the favourableness of the disposition towards the entity being disparaged, and varies directly with the favourableness of the disposition towards the entity disparaging it. 'Appreciation should be maximal when our friends humiliate our enemies, and minimal when the enemies manage to get the upper hand over our friends' (p.101).

A study by Zillmann and Cantor (1972) supporting their dispositional model used cartoons and jokes depicting encounters between a superior and a subordinate. In different conditions the superior and the subordinate, who were represented as father and son, professor and student, and employer and employee, had the final word, so becoming dominant in the encounter. Subjects were students and professional businessmen, and the results indicated that students gave higher funniness ratings to the cartoons and jokes in which the subordinate disparaged his superior, rather than the reverse. Conversely professionals gave higher ratings to those in which the subordinate was disparaged by his superior, suggesting that, if subjects have more sympathy for, and empathy with, those who have similar experiences to themselves, then the dispositional theory is supported.

A more complex superiority theory has been proposed by La Fave (e.g. La Fave, 1972, 1977; La Fave, McCarthy and Haddad, 1973; La Fave, Haddad and Maesen, 1976). In this version reference groups, or identification classes, are included so as to state the theory in attitudinal terms. For example La Fave *et al.* (1973) demonstrated that pro-Canadian Canadians preferred jokes in which a Canadian disparaged an American rather than the reverse.

The incorporation of an analysis of attitudes by use of reference groups to superiority theories has been a useful contribution in so far as it allows the examination of jokes directed against ethnic groups (e.g. Bourhis, Gadfield, Giles and Tajfel, 1977; Mutuma, La Fave, Mannell and Guilmette, 1977), and in that it allows an experimenter to check subjects' actual affiliations with the protagonists in the humour. For example, Bourhis *et al.* demonstrated that Welsh teenagers (living in Wales, being Welsh-born, and describing themselves as being 'very Welsh') did not appreciate anti-Welsh jokes, but reacted to anti-English jokes more favourably when the joke was told in an English rather than a Welsh accent, and when the intergroup context was made salient, by preliminary essay writing on the 'ways in which the Welsh way of life had suffered through English supremacy in Wales' (p.262).

La Fave's work and that following from it has been considered only briefly here. It is clear that, in view of the prevalence of ethnic jokes, the connection between humour and attitudes is an important one. It has not yet been fully explored, however. Losco and Epstein (1975) claimed to have found a subtle measure of attitudes by use of humour preference for cartoons, but nevertheless admitted that the relationship is far from straightforward. It would appear to be another field which social psychology could fruitfully explore.

The superiority theories have not gone unchallenged in spite of their apparent applications in the more applied aspects of social psychology. Suls (1977) pointed out that they fail to explain the essential aspects of humour: why we do not laugh at other non-humorous incidents of disparagement. It may be, as suggested by Zillmann and Cantor (1976), that a joke setting is required. Further, these theories cannot explain all types of humour, only those including disparagement. Suls proposed that superiority theories can be conceptualized in terms of incongruity and resolution. In this case the punch line of an ethnic joke provides the necessary resolution only if the subject has the required information to understand the disparagement implied. If, for example, he is a member of the disparaged group he may not be able to perceive the punch line as a satisfactory resolution, and the joke should not seem amusing to him. Suls therefore suggests how superiority theories may be incorporated into the broader incongruity model, while still maintaining that the variables they propose are neither trivial nor irrelevant.

(iv) *Non-incongruity theories of humour: a conclusion*

As stated earlier the theories explaining humour without using the concept of congruity might be expected to be a somewhat mixed collection. They can broadly be divided into those attempting to explain the function of humour, either in terms of aggressive and sexual impulses (Freud) or in terms of social interaction (Kane *et al.*, 1977; Martineau, 1972), and those which are more concerned with its construction and analysis, (Berlyne, 1972; La Fave *et al.*, 1976; Zillmann and Cantor, 1976). Of the former group Freud's theory of humour is an offshoot of his more general work on psychoanalysis, and should be regarded more as a source of ideas than as a source of experimental hypotheses. Those models suggesting the function of humour to be in aiding social interaction have produced little concrete evidence so far, although that of Kane *et al.* promises to be fruitful in this respect.

It is remarkable that the non-incongruity theories which deal with the construction of jokes have both been recently reinterpreted in terms of incongruity. It has been suggested by Rothbart (1977) that arousal theory, and by Suls (1977) that superiority theories, can be equally well understood by use of incongruity models. This, in itself, is encouraging for proponents of incongruity theory, but it is possible to be even more emphatic in its support. As discussed earlier, arousal is a term which certain psychologists (e.g. Andrew, 1974) find of dubious explanatory value, and if one accepts this view then Rothbart's proposal that arousal and incongruity are similar explanatory mechanisms at different levels of abstraction is inadequate. They may indeed be at different levels of abstraction, but in terms of the sufficiency of the explanation they offer, incongruity theories seem superior. With regard to superiority theories, these, as Suls has pointed out, may be subsumed under an incongruity framework which is more inclusive than other models. In the light of these arguments it appears that there is no very serious challenge to incongruity theories of humour.

(b) *Inconsistency and negative self esteem*

At the beginning of the chapter it was suggested that consistency allows us to predict other people's behaviour and to have positive self esteem when we demonstrate consistency ourselves. Both functions contribute to social behaviour in that being able to anticipate others' behaviour enables us to adapt our own. Further, consistency appears to be a valued trait particularly in ourselves, and a number of clinicians (e.g. Rogers, 1950, 1959) have claimed that it results from positive self esteem which is essential for mental health.

This section will briefly consider the meaning of self esteem and how various theorists have related its absence (or low self esteem) to psychopathology. It is not intended that this discussion should be comprehensive since that would be beyond the scope of this book. The intention is merely to demonstrate that negative or low self esteem is an aspect of psychopathology which may be responsible at least in part, for inconsistent behaviour.

In discussing the meaning of the concept of self esteem one is immediately hampered by the different uses and terms given to it by different theorists. Wells and Marwell (1976) conclude that most terms, such as self-love, self-acceptance (or rejection), self appraisal, self-worth, sense of adequacy, ego strength, 'denote some basic process of psychological functioning which can be described as either self-evaluation or self-affection or as some combination of the two' (p.7). A rather different emphasis is evident in the claim by Ziller (1973) that the concept is usually taken as the individual's perception of his own worth, but in terms of a social frame of reference provided by significant others. In Ziller's theory self esteem is 'not absolute, but evolves from a series of self-other comparisons, or, exists only in a social context' (p.6). According to this view (Ziller, Hagey, Smith and Long, 1969) a person with low self esteem does not possess a well-developed conceptual buffer for evaluative stimuli, and is field dependent (Witkin, Dyk, Faterson, Goodenough and Karp, 1962). He will be readily influenced by the immediate social environment, and since his behaviour is not mediated and integrated by a strong self concept or internal guidance mechanism it will tend to be inconsistent with subsequent behaviour.

Ziller demonstrated, by a number of studies, the occurrence of low self esteem in certain psychiatric patients. For example, Ziller, Megas and DeCencio (1964) showed that acutely depressed patients who had been administered electroconvulsive shock therapy had lower self esteem than less severely depressed patients who had not received this treatment. In the same study neuropsychiatric patients were compared with hospital staff showing again that the patients had lower self esteem. Similar findings were demonstrated by Ziller and Grossman (1967).

A different approach is provided by Rosenberg (1964, 1965) and Rosenberg and Simmons (1971), who suggest that self esteem is an evaluative attitude. Their main concern is the development of adolescent self esteem particularly in relation to family characteristics and race. More relevant for the present discussion is Rosenberg's (1965) suggestion that people with low self esteem show more neurotic tendencies, have greater difficulty in social interaction and have lower expectations and aspirations for success than do those with high self esteem. Coopersmith (1967) takes a somewhat similar approach to Rosenberg and concludes that the development of high self esteem in children is a result of parents being accepting, and enforcing clearly defined limits yet respecting individual initiative within those limits.

Neo-Freudian analysts, whilst rarely being concerned with self esteem as such, often developed concepts akin to it and may have influenced later writers. Adler (1930) for example, claimed that all people to some extent tend towards a feeling of inferiority which results in an effort to counteract this by striving for superiority. Horney (1950) maintained that individuals want to be valued by themselves and by others, and that this need for security is the result of basic anxiety formed from the child's experience of helplessness. Sullivan (1953) emphasized a more socially orientated approach, suggesting that the self, having no inborn component, develops in childhood as a result of reinforcement when the child interacts with parents. In Sullivan's theory the self-system includes self-evaluation and develops through learning so that anxiety is minimal. Fromm (1939) proposed a similarly social theory, stressing that a person's self esteem (self-love in his terminology) is a prerequisite for competent social behaviour and the ability to love others.

While the above discussion indicates that a number of writers have seen self esteem as important for mental health, Rogers (e.g. 1950, 1951, 1959) has been the most emphatic in this respect. The central construct of Roger's theory is the self, and 'self acceptance', a further important concept, was described as an affective judgment about the self. For Rogers the self was a perceived object in a phenomenal field, a type of *Gestalt* pattern of related perceptions. When there is a discrepancy between the self as it is perceived, and the way the rest of experience is perceived – for example, if another person makes a judgment about oneself which conflicts with one's self concept, then incongruence (or inconsistency) results. This inconsistency can lead to a state of confusion and tension leading to some experiences being denied to awareness or distorted in awareness, since Rogers contends that a person will attempt to maintain a consistent or congruent self concept.

A further emphasis in the theory, and in the client-centred therapy resulting from it, is on unconditional positive regard. A child will only develop self acceptance or self esteem if he is given unconditional positive regard – that is, if he is valued for himself. If positive regard is conditional on fulfilling certain criteria then the child may adopt various defences against seeing himself in particular ways. For example, denial or distortion in awareness may be adopted, and can lead to problems in social interaction with others. Rogers's client-centred therapy includes the therapist being warm and accepting towards the patient (the client, in Rogers's terminology), in other words giving him unconditional positive regard. This approach leads the patient to self acceptance and to more consistent behaviour.

The relevance of Rogers's work for the present discussion is apparent: lack of self acceptance, or low self esteem leads to the adoption of defences which are characteristic of psychopathology and which in turn leads to inconsistent behaviour.

More empirical evidence of this relationship has been provided by Yochelson and Samenow (1976) who use the concept of fragmentation to describe a type of criminal thinking pattern which portrays inconsistency between attitudes and behaviour. A typical example might be that criminals honour and respect their mothers in terms of their attitudes towards them, yet their behaviour causes grief for their mothers. This fragmentation or inconsistency between attitudes and behaviour allows the maintenance of a positive self concept, in the face of contradictory evidence: a person can merely ignore the negative aspects which would characterize his self concept. While inconsistency between attitudes and behaviour is not uncommon (see Chapter 2), it is the extent to which it occurs in criminals which leads to what may be considered pathological behaviour. Such evidence, together with the work of Rogers, supports the argument that consistency, mediated by self esteem, is strongly related to normally adaptive behaviour.

3 Conclusion: when consistency fails

This chapter has discussed two main aspects of inconsistent behaviour. The first, when behaviour is intentionally not predictable included role-playing, literature and, in the main body of the chapter, humour. The second aspect of inconsistency has been related to negative self esteem and to pathological behaviour.

Both are unusual aspects of social behaviour. There remains, however, a third possibility which is even more exceptional. When behaviour is unintentionally not predictable, it may be extremely pathological, but of necessity it will be asocial. If other people cannot predict our behaviour they cannot interact with us.

In conclusion, then, it seems that consistency, in all its facets, is a cognitive mechanism that allows prediction of behaviour, by allowing some social information to be redundant. It therefore allows behaviour to be social, and could well form the foundation of social psychology and of society.

Bibliography

Abelson, R.P. and Rosenber, M.J. (1958), 'Symbolic psychologic: a model of attitudinal cognition', *Behavioral Science, 3*, 1-13.

Aderman, D. (1969), 'Effects of anticipating future interaction on the preference for balanced states', *Journal of Personality and Social Psychology, 11*, 214-19.

Adler, A. (1930), 'Individual Psychology', in C. Murchison (ed.), *Psychologies of 1930*, Clark University Press, Worcester, Mass.

Adorno, T.W., Frenkel-Brunswik, E., Levinson, D.J., and Sanford, R.N. (1950), *The Authoritarian Personality*, Harper & Row, New York.

Ajzen, I. and Fishbein, M. (1972), 'Attitudes and normative beliefs as factors influencing behavioral intentions', *Journal of Personality and Social Psychology, 21*, 1-9.

Alexander, C.N. Jr, Zucker, L.G. and Brody, C.L. (1970), 'Experimental expectations and autokinetic experiences; consistency theories and judgmental convergence', *Sociometry, 33*, 108-22.

Allport, G.W. (1935), 'Attitudes', in C.M. Murchison (ed.), *Handbook of Social Psychology*, Clark University Press, Worcester, Mass.

Allport, G.W. (1937), *Personality: A Psychological Interpretation*, Holt, New York.

Allport, G.W. and Odbert, H.S. (1936), 'Trait-names. A psycholexical study', *Psychological Monographs, 47* (whole No.211).

Anderson, N.H. (1962), 'Application of an additive model to impression formation', *Science, 138*, 817-18.

Anderson, N.H. (1965), 'Averaging versus adding as a stimulus combination rule in impression formation', *Journal of Experimental Psychology, 70*, 394-400.

Andrew, R. (1974), 'Arousal and the causation of behaviour', *Behaviour L.I.*, 10-163.

Andrews, I.R. and Johnson, D.L. (1971), 'Small group polarization of judgments', *Psychonomic Science, 24*, 191-92.

Argyle, M. and Little, B.R. (1972), 'Do Personality Traits apply to

Social Behaviour?', *Journal for the Theory of Social Behaviour, 2,* 1-35.

Armistead, N. (ed.) (1974), *Reconstructing Social Psychology,* Penguin, Harmondsworth.

Aronson, E. (1968), 'Dissonance Theory: Progress and Problems', in R.P. Abelson, E. Aronson, W.J. McGuire, T.M. Newcomb, M.J. Rosenberg and P.H. Tannenbaum (eds), *Theories of Cognitive Consistency: a Sourcebook,* Rand McNally, Chicago.

Asch, S.E. (1946), 'Forming impressions of personality', *Journal of Abnormal and Social Psychology, 41,* 258-90.

Asch, S.E. (1956), 'Studies of independence and conformity: A minority of one against a unanimous majority', *Psychological Monographs, 70,* no. 9, whole no. 416.

Bandler, R.J., Madaras, G.R. and Bem, D.J. (1968), 'Self-observation as a source of pain perception', *Journal of Personality and Social Psychology, 9,* 205-9.

Baron, R.A., Byrne, D. and Griffitt, W. (1974), *Social Psychology: Understanding Human Interaction,* Allyn & Bacon, Boston.

Beattie, J. (1776), 'Essay on laughter and ludicrous composition', in *Essays,* Edinburgh.

Bem, D.J. (1965), 'An experimental analysis of self-persuasion', *Journal of Experimental Social Psychology, 1,* 199-218.

Bem, D.J. (1967), 'An alternative interpretation of cognitive dissonance phenomena', *Psychological Review, 74,* 183-200.

Bennion, R.C. (1961), 'Task, trial by trial score variability of internal versus external control of reinforcement', unpublished doctoral dissertation, Ohio State University.

Berger, S.M. (1962), 'Conditioning through vicarious instigation', *Psychological Review, 69,* 450-66.

Berlyne, D.E. (1960), *Conflict, Arousal, and Curiosity,* McGraw Hill, Chicago.

Berlyne, D.E. (1967), 'Arousal and reinforcement', *Nebraska Symposium on Motivation,* 1-110.

Berlyne, D.E. (1969a), 'Laughter, humour and play', in G. Lindzey and E. Aronson (eds), *Handbook of Social Psychology* (2nd ed) vol. 3, Addison-Wesley, Mass.

Berlyne, D.E. (1969b), 'The reward value of indifferent stimulation', in J.T. Tapp and G.W. Meier (eds), *Reinforcement,* Academic Press, New York.

Berlyne, D.E. (1972), 'Humour and its kin', in J.H. Goldstein and P.E. McGhee (eds), *The Psychology of Humour,* Academic Press, New York.

Bermann, E. and Miller, D.R. (1967), 'The matching of mates', in R. Jessor and S. Feshbach (eds), *Cognition, Personality and Clinical Psychology,* Jossey-Bass, San Francisco.

Berscheid, E., Dion, K., Walster, E. and Walster, G.W. (1971), 'Physical attractiveness and dating choice: A test of the matching hypothesis', *Journal of Experimental Social Psychology, 7,* 173-89.

Berscheid, E. and Walster, E. (1974), 'A little bit about love', in T.L. Huston (ed.), *Foundations of Interpersonal Attraction,* Academic Press, New York.

Bettelheim, B. (1978), *The Uses of Enchantment: The Meaning and Importance of Fairy Tales,* Penguin, Harmondsworth.

Billig, M. (1976), *Social Psychology and Intergroup Relations,* Academic Press, London.

Billig, M. (1977), 'The new social psychology and "fascism"', *European Journal of Social Psychology, 7,* 393-432.

Billig, M. and Tajfel, H. (1973), 'Social categorization and similarity in intergroup behaviour', *European Journal of Social Psychology, 3,* 27-52.

Blake, R.R. and Mouton, J.S. (1962), 'Over-evaluation of own group's products in intergroup competition', *Journal of Abnormal and Social Psychology, 64,* 237-8.

Blascovich, J., Ginsberg, G.P. and Veach, T.L. (1975), 'A pluralistic explanation of choice shifts on the risk dimension', *Journal of Personality and Social Psychology, 31,* 422-9.

Blumberg, H.H. (1969), 'On being liked more than you like', *Journal of Personality and Social Psychology, 11,* 121-8.

Blumer, H. (1969), *Symbolic Interactionism: Perspective and Method,* Prentice-Hall, Englewood Cliffs, N.J.

Bourhis, R.Y., Gadfield, N.J., Giles, H. and Tajfel, H. (1977), 'Context and ethnic humour in intergroup relations', in A.J. Chapman and H.C. Foot (eds), *It's a Funny Thing, Humour,* Pergamon, Oxford.

Bowerman, C.E. and Day, B. (1965), 'A test of the theory of complementary needs as applied to couples during courtship', *American Sociological Review, 21,* 602-5.

Bowers, K.S. (1973), 'Situationism in Psychology: An analysis and a critique', *Psychological Review, 80,* 307-36.

Branthwaite, A. and Jones, J.E. (1975), 'Fairness and discrimination: English versus Welsh', *European Journal of Social Psychology, 5,* 323-38.

Briggs, K.M. (1970), *A Dictionary of British Folk Tales,* Indiana University Press, Bloomington.

Brown, R. (1965), *Social Psychology,* Free Press, New York.

Burnstein, E. and Vinokur, A. (1973), 'Testing two classes of theories about group-induced shifts in individual choice', *Journal of Experimental Social Psychology, 9,* 123-37.

Burnstein, E., Vinokur, A. and Trope, V. (1973), 'Interpersonal comparison versus persuasive argumentation: a more direct test of alternative explanations for group induced shifts in individual choice', *Journal of Experimental Social Psychology, 9,* 236-45.

Burnstein, E., Vinokur, A. and Pichevin, M.F. (1974), 'What do differences between own, admired and attributed choices have to do with group induced shifts in choice?', *Journal of Experimental Social Psychology, 10,* 428-43.

Burnstein, E. and Vinokur, A. (1977), 'Persuasive argumentation and social comparison as determinants of attitude polarization', *Journal of Experimental Social Psychology, 13,* 315-32.

Butterfield, E.C. (1964), 'Locus of control, test anxiety, reaction to frustration and achievement attitudes', *Journal of Personality, 32,* 298-311.

Byrne, D. (1961a), 'Interpersonal attraction and attitude similarity', *Journal of Abnormal and Social Psychology, 62,* 713-15.

Byrne, D. (1961b), 'The influence of propinquity and opportunities for interaction on classroom relationships', *Human Relations, 14,* 63-9.

Byrne, D. (1962), 'Response to attitude similarity – dissimilarity as a function of affiliation need', *Journal of Personality, 30,* 164-77.

Byrne, D. (1964), 'Repression–sensitization as a dimension of personality', in B.A. Maher (ed.), *Progress in Experimental Personality Research,* Academic Press, New York, pp. 169-220.

Byrne, D. (1969), 'Attitudes and attraction', in L. Berkowitz (ed.), *Advances in Experimental Social Psychology,* vol. 4, Academic Press, New York.

Byrne, D. and Buehler, J.A. (1955), 'A note on the influence of propinquity upon acquaintanceships', *Journal of Abnormal and Social Psychology, 51,* 147-8.

Byrne, D. and Nelson, D. (1965), 'Attraction as a linear function of proportion of positive reinforcements', *Journal of Personality and Social Psychology, 1,* 659-63.

Byrne, D. and Clore, G.L. (1966), 'Predicting interpersonal attraction toward strangers presented in three different stimulus modes', *Psychonomic Science, 4,* 239-40.

Byrne, D., Young, R.K. and Griffitt, W. (1966), 'The reinforcement properties of attitude statements', *Journal of Experimental Research in Personality, 1,* 266-76.

Byrne, D. and Clore, G.L. (1967), 'Effectance arousal and attraction', *Journal of Personality and Social Psychology Monograph, 6* (4, Whole No. 638).

Byrne, D., Griffitt, W. and Stefaniak, D. (1967), 'Attraction and similarity of personality characteristics', *Journal of Personality and Social Psychology, 5,* 89-90.

Campbell, D.T. (1969), 'Prospective: artifact and control', in Rosenthal R. and Rosnow, R.L. (eds), *Artifact in Behaviour Research,* Academic Press, New York.

Chapanis, N.J. and Chapanis, A.C. (1964), 'Cognitive dissonance: Five years later', *Psychological Bulletin, 61,* 1-22.

Chapman, A.J. (1973), 'Social facilitation of laughter in children', *Journal of Experimental Social Psychology, 9,* 528-41.

Chapman, A.J. (1975), 'Humourous laughter in children', *Journal of Personality and Social Psychology, 31,* 42-9.
Christie, R. and Cook, P. (1958), 'A guide to published literature relating to the authoritarian personality through 1956', *Journal of Psychology, 45,* 171-99.
Codol, J.-P. (1975), 'On the so-called "superior conformity of the self" behaviour: Twenty experimental investigations'. *European Journal of Social Psychology, 5,* 457-501.
Coopersmith, S. (1967), *The Antecedents of Self-Esteem,* Freeman, San Francisco.
Cottrell, N.B. (1975), 'Heider's Structural Balance Principle as a Conceptual Rule', *Journal of Personality and Social Psychology, 31,* 713-20.
Cottrell, N.B., Ingraham, L.H. and Monfort, F.W. (1971), 'The retention of balanced and imbalanced cognitive structures', *Journal of Personality, 39,* 112-31.
Crano, W.D. and Cooper, R.E. (1973), 'Examination of Newcomb's extensions of structural balance theory', *Journal of Personality and Social Psychology, 27,* 344-53.
Crockett, W.H. (1974), 'Balance, agreement and subjective evaluations of the P-O-X triads', *Journal of Personality and Social Psychology, 29,* 102-10.
Crowne, D.P. and Marlowe, D.A. (1960), 'A new scale of social desirability independent of psychopathology', *Journal of Consulting Psychology, 24,* 349-54.
Darley, J.M. and Berscheid, E. (1967), 'Increased liking as a result of the anticipation of personal contact', *Human Relations, 20,* 29-39.
Darley, J.M. and Latané, B. (1968), 'Bystander intervention in emergencies: diffusion of responsibility', *Journal of Personality and Social Psychology, 8,* 377-83.
Davison, G.G. and Valins, S. (1969), 'Maintenance of self-attributed and drug-attributed behaviour change', *Journal of Personality and Social Psychology, 11,* 25-33.
Deutsch, M. (1949), 'The directions of behaviour: a field-theoretical approach to the understanding of inconsistencies', *Journal of Social Issues, 5,* 43-9.
Deutsch, M. and Gerard, H.B. (1955), 'A study of normative and informational social influences upon individual judgement', *Journal of Abnormal and Social Psychology, 51,* 629-36.
Deutsch, M. and Krauss, R.M. (1960), 'The effect of threat upon interpersonal bargaining', *Journal of Abnormal and Social Psychology, 61,* 181-9.
Deutsch, M. and Solomon, L. (1959), 'Reactions to evaluations of others as influenced by self-evaluations', *Sociometry, 22,* 93-112.
Doise, W. (1969), 'Intergroup relations and polarization of individual and collective judgments', *Journal of Personality and Social Psychology, 12,* 136-43.
Doise, W. and Sinclair, A. (1973), 'The categorization process in

intergroup relations', *European Journal of Social Psychology, 3,* 145-57.

Dollard, J., Doob, L.W., Miller, N.E., Mowrer, O.H. and Sears, R.R. (1939), *Frustration and Aggression,* Yale University Press, New Haven, Conn.

Duck, S.W. (1973), *Personal Relationships and Personal Constructs: A Study of Friendship Formation,* Wiley, London.

Duck, S.W. (1977), *The Study of Acquaintance,* Saxon House (Teakfields), London.

Duck, S.W. and Spencer, C.P. (1972), 'Personal constructs and friendship formation', *Journal of Personality and Social Psychology, 23,* 40-5.

Duck, S.W. and Craig, G. (1978), 'Personality similarity and the development of friendship: a longitudinal study', *British Journal of Social and Clinical Psychology, 17,* 237-42.

Dutton, D.G. (1972), 'Effect of feedback parameters on congruency versus positivity effects in reactions to personal evaluations', *Journal of Personality and Social Psychology, 24,* 366-71.

Ebbeson, E.B. and Bowers, R.J. (1974), 'Proportion of risky to conservative arguments in a group discussion and choice shift', *Journal of Personality and Social Psychology, 29,* 316-27.

Edelmann, R.J. and Hampson, S.E. (1979), 'Changes in non-verbal behaviour during embarrassment', *British Journal of Social and Clinical Psychology, 18,* 385-90.

Eiser, J.R. (1971a), 'Categorization, cognitive consistency and the concept of dimensional salience', *European Journal of Social Psychology, 1,* 435-54.

Eiser, J.R. (1971b), 'Enhancement of contrast in the absolute judgment of attitude statements', *Journal of Personality and Social Psychology, 17,* 1-10.

Eiser, J.R. (1975), 'Attitudes and the use of evaluative language: a two-way process', *Journal for the Theory of Social Behaviour, 5,* 235-48.

Eiser, J.R. (1979), 'Interpersonal attribution', in H. Tajfel and C. Fraser (eds), *Introducing Social Psychology,* Penguin, Harmondsworth.

Eiser, J.R. (1980), *Cognitive Social Psychology: A Guidebook to Theory and Research*, McGraw-Hill, London.

Eiser, J.R. and Mower White, C.J. (1974a), 'Evaluative consistency and social judgment', *Journal of Personality and Social Psychology, 30,* 349-59.

Eiser, J.R. and Mower White, C.J. (1974b), 'The persuasiveness of labels: Attitude change produced through definition of the attitude continuum', *European Journal of Social Psychology, 4,* 89-92.

Eiser, J.R. and Mower White, C.J. (1975), 'Categorization and congruity in attitudinal judgment', *Journal of Personality and Social Psychology, 31,* 769-75.

Eiser, J.R. and Stroebe, W. (1972), *Categorization and Social Judgment,* Academic Press, London.

Eiser, J.R. and Ross, M. (1977), 'Partisan language, immediacy and attitude change', *European Journal of Social Psychology, 7,* 477-89.

Endler, N.S. (1973), 'The person vs the situation – a pseudo issue? A response to Alker', *Journal of Personality, 41,* 287-303.

Eysenck, H.J. (1961), 'The Effects of Psychotherapy', in H.J. Eysenck (ed.), *Handbook of Abnormal Psychology: An Experimental Approach,* Basic Books, New York.

Eysenck, H.J. and Wilson, G.D. (1973), *The Experimental Study of Freudian Theories,* Methuen, London.

Farr, R.M. (1977), 'Heider, Harré and Herzlich on health and illness: Some observations on the structure of "representations collectives"', *European Journal of Social Psychology, 7,* 491-504.

Fazio, R.H., Zanna, M.P. and Cooper, J. (1977), 'Dissonance and self-perception; an integrative view of each theory's proper domain of application', *Journal of Experimental Social Psychology, 13,* 464-79.

Feather, N.T. (1961), 'The relationship of persistence at a task to expectation of success and achievement-related motives', *Journal of Abnormal and Social Psychology, 63,* 552-61.

Feather, N.T. (1967), 'Some personality correlates of external control', *Australian Journal of Psychology, 19,* 253-60.

Felipe, A. (1970), 'Evaluative vs Descriptive consistency in Trait Inferences', *Journal of Personality and Social Psychology, 16,* 627-38.

Festinger, L. (1950),'Laboratory experiments: The role of group belongingness', in J.G. Miller (ed.), *Experiments in Social Progress,* McGraw-Hill, New York.

Festinger, L. (1954), 'A theory of social comparison processes', *Human Relations, 7,* 117-40.

Festinger, L. (1957), *A Theory of Cognitive Dissonance*, Row, Peterson, Evanston, Ill.

Festinger, L., Riecken, H.W. and Schachter, S. (1956), *When Prophecy Fails,* University of Minneapolis Press.

Festinger, L. and Carlsmith, J.M. (1959), 'Cognitive consequences of forced compliance', *Journal of Abnormal and Social Psychology, 58,* 203-10.

Festinger, L., Schachter, S. and Back, K. (1950), *Social Pressures in Informal Groups: A Study of a Housing Community,* Harper, New York.

Fishbein, M. (1967), 'Attitude and the prediction of behaviour', in M. Fishbein (ed.), *Readings in Attitude Theory and Measurement,* Wiley, New York.

Fishbein, M. and Ajzen, I. (1975), *Belief, Attitude, Intention and Behaviour: An Introduction to Theory and Research*, Addison-Wesley, Reading, Mass.

Fiske, D.W. and Maddi, S.R. (1961), *Functions of Varied Experience,* Dorsey, Homewood Ill.

Foot, H.C. and Chapman, A.J. (1976), 'The social responsiveness of young children in humourous situations', in A.J. Chapman and H.C. Foot (eds), *Humour and Laughter: Theory, Research and Applications,* Wiley, London.

Forgas, J.P. (1977), 'Polarization and moderation of person perception judgments as a function of group interaction style', *European Journal of Social Psychology, 7,* 175-87.

Fraser, C., Gouge, C. and Billig, M. (1971), 'Risky shift, cautious shifts and group polarization', *European Journal of Social Psychology, 1,* 7-30.

Freud, S. (1900), *The Interpretation of Dreams,* (trans. 1976) Pelican Freud Library, vol. 4, Penguin, Harmondsworth.

Freud, S. (1905), *Der Witz and seine Beziehung zum Unbewussten,* Deuticke, Leipzig and Vienna; trans. *Jokes and their Relation to the Unconscious,* Norton, New York, 1960.

Freud, S. (1928), 'Humour', *International Journal of Psychoanalysis, 9,* 1-6.

Freud, S. (1933), *New Introductory Lectures on Psychoanalysis,* Pelican Freud Library, vol. 2, Penguin, Harmondsworth.

Fromm, E. (1939), 'Selfishness and self-love', *Psychiatry: Journal for the Study of Interpersonal Processes, 2,* 507-23.

Fuller, C.H. (1974), 'Comparison of two experimental paradigms as tests of Heider's Balance Theory', *Journal of Personality and Social Psychology, 30,* 802-6.

Garfinkel, H. (1967), *Studies in Ethnomethodology,* Prentice-Hall, Englewood Cliffs, NJ.

Gerard, H.B. and Fleischer, L. (1967), 'Recall and pleasantness of balanced and imbalanced cognitive structures', *Journal of Personality and Social Psychology, 7,* 332-7.

Gerard, H.B. and Hoyt, M.F. (1974), 'Distinctiveness of social categorization and attitude toward ingroup members', *Journal of Personality and Social Psychology, 29,* 836-42.

Gergen, K. (1973), 'Social psychology as history', *Journal of Personality and Social Psychology, 26,* 309-20.

Giles, H. and Oxford, G.S. (1970), 'Towards a multidimensional theory of laughter causation and its social implications', *Bulletin of the British Psychological Society, 23,* 97-105.

Glixman, A.F. (1967), 'Psychology of the scientist XXII. Effects of examiner, examiner-sex and subject sex upon categorizing behaviour', *Perceptual and Motor Skills, 24,* 107-17.

Godkewitsch, M. (1976), 'Physiological and verbal indices of arousal in rated humour', in A.J. Chapman and H.C. Foot (eds), *Humour and Laughter: Theory, Research and Applications,* Wiley, London.

Goodman, M.E. (1964), *Race Awareness in Young Children,* Collier

Books, New York.

Gordon, R. (1976), 'Ethnomethodology: a radical critique', *Human Relations, 29,* 193-202.

Greenwald, A.B. (1975), 'On the inconclusiveness of "crucial" cognitive tests of dissonance versus self-perception theories', *Journal of Experimental Social Psychology, 11,* 490-9.

Grossman, S.A. (1977), 'The use of jokes in psychotherapy', in A.J. Chapman and H.C. Foot (eds), *It's a Funny Thing, Humour,* Pergamon, Oxford.

Gullahorn, J.T. (1952), 'Distance and friendship as factors in the gross interaction matrix', *Sociometry, 15,* 123-34.

Gutman, G. and Knox, R. (1972), 'Balance, agreement and attraction in pleasantness, tension and consistency ratings of hypothetical social situations', *Journal of Personality and Social Psychology, 24,* 351-7.

Hampson, S.E. (1982), *The Construction of Personality: An introduction to experimental personality research*, Routledge & Kegan Paul, London.

Harré, R. and Secord, P.F. (1972), *The Explanation of Social Behaviour,* Blackwell, Oxford.

Heider, F. (1944), 'Social perception and phenomenal causality', *Psychological Review, 51,* 358-74.

Heider, F. (1946), 'Attitudes and cognitive organization', *Journal of Psychology, 21,* 107-12.

Heider, F. (1958), *The Psychology of Interpersonal Relations,* Wiley, New York.

Helson, H. (1964), *Adaptation-Level Theory,* Harper & Row, New York.

Herzlich, C. (1973), *Health and Illness: a Social-psychological Analysis,* Academic Press, London.

Hewitt, J. and Goldman, M. (1974), 'Self-esteem, need for approval, and reactions to personal evaluations', *Journal of Experimental Social Psychology, 10,* 201-10.

Hilkevitch, R.R. (1960), 'Social interaction processes: A quantitative study', *Psychological Reports, 7,* 195-201.

Hinckley, E.D. (1932), 'The influence of individual opinion on construction of an attitude scale', *Journal of Social Psychology, 3,* 283-96.

Hindess, B. (1973), *The Uses of Official Statistics in Sociology,* Macmillan, London.

Hobbes, T. (1651), *Leviathan* (republished 1968), Penguin, Harmondsworth.

Homans, G.C. (1961), *Social Behaviour: Its Elementary Forms,* Harcourt, Brace & World, New York.

Horney, K. (1950), *Neurosis and Human Growth,* Norton, New York.

Hovland, C.I. and Sherif, M. (1952), 'Judgmental phenomena and scales of attitude measurement: Item displacement in

Thurstone scales', *Journal of Abnormal and Social Psychology, 47,* 822-32.

Hovland, C.I. and Weiss, W. (1952), 'Influence of source credulity on communication effectiveness', *Public Opinion Quarterly, 15,* 635-50.

Huston, T.L. (1973), 'Ambiguity of acceptance, social desirability and dating choice', *Journal of Experimental Social Psychology, 9,* 32-42.

Hyman, H.H. and Sheatsley, P.B. (1954), '"The Authoritarian Personality" – A methodological critique', in R. Christie and M. Jahoda (eds), *Studies in the Scope and Method of 'The Authoritarian Personality',* Free Press, New York.

Inglis, I.R. (1975), 'Exploratory behaviour of the hooded rat', unpublished PhD thesis, University of Bristol.

Insko, C.A., Songer, E. and McGarvey, W. (1974), 'Balance, positivity and agreement in the Jordan paradigm: A defence of Balance Theory', *Journal of Experimental Social Psychology, 10,* 53-83.

Izard, C. (1960), 'Personality similarity and friendship', *Journal of Abnormal and Social Psychology, 61,* 47-51.

Jahoda, M. (1972), 'Social Psychology and Psychoanalysis: A mutual challenge', *Bulletin of the British Psychological Society, 25,* 269-74.

Jellison, J.M. and Riskind, J.A. (1971), 'Attribution of risk to others as a function of their ability', *Journal of Personality and Social Psychology, 20,* 413-15.

Jennings, H.H. (1943), *Leadership and Isolation,* Longmans, Green, New York.

Jones, E.E. and Davis, K.E. (1965), 'From Acts to Dispositions: The attribution process in person perception', in L. Berkowitz (ed.), *Advances in Experimental Social Psychology, 2,* Academic Press, New York.

Jones, E.E. and Harris, V.A. (1967), 'The attribution of Attitudes', *Journal of Experimental Social Psychology, 3,* 1-24.

Jones, E.E. and Goethals, G.R. (1971), 'Order effects in Impression Formation. Attribution context and the nature of the entity', in E.E. Jones, D.E. Kanouse, H.H. Kelley, R.E. Nisbett, S. Valins and B. Weiner, (eds), *Attribution: Perceiving the Causes of Behaviour,* General Learning Press, Morristown.

Jones, E.E. and Nisbett, R.E. (1971), 'The Actor and the Observer: Divergent Perceptions of the Causes of Behavior', in E.E. Jones, D.E. Kanouse, H.H. Kelley, R.E. Nisbett, S. Valins and B. Weiner (eds), *Attribution: Perceiving Causes of Behavior,* General Learning Press, Morristown.

Jones, E.E., Rock, L., Shaver, K.G., Goethals, G.R. and Ward, L.M. (1968), 'Pattern of Performance and Ability Attribution: An unexpected primary effect', *Journal of Personality and Social Psychology, 10,* 317-40.

Jones, E.E., Worchel, S., Goethals, G.R. and Grumet, J.F. (1971),

'Prior expectancy and behavioral extremity as determinants of attitude attribution', *Journal of Experimental Social Psychology, 7,* 59-80.

Jordan, N. (1953), 'Behavioural forces that are a function of attitudes and cognitive organization', *Human Relations, 6,* 273-87.

Kane, T.R., Suls, J. and Tedeschi, J.T. (1977), 'Humour as a Tool of Social Interaction', in A.J. Chapman and H.C. Foot (eds), *It's a Funny Thing, Humour,* Pergamon, Oxford.

Kanouse, D.E. (1971), 'Language, labeling and attribution', in E.E. Jones, D.E. Kanouse, H.H. Kelley, R.E. Nisbett, S. Valins, and B. Weiner (eds), *Attribution: Perceiving the Causes of Behavior,* General Learning Press, Morristown.

Katz, I. (1967), 'The socialization of academic motivation in minority group children', in D. Levine (ed.), *Nebraska Symposium on Motivation,* University of Nebraska.

Keith-Spiegel, P. (1972), 'Early conceptions of humour: varieties and issues', in J.H. Goldstein and P.E. McGhee (eds), *The Psychology of Humour,* Academic Press, New York.

Kelley, H.H. (1967), 'Attribution Theory in Social Psychology', in D. Levine (ed.) *Nebraska Symposium on Motivation, 15,* 192-238.

Kelly, G.A. (1955), *The Psychology of Personal Constructs,* Vol. I, Norton, New York.

Kerchoff, A.C. and Davis, K.I. (1962), 'Value consensus and need complementarity in mate selection', *American Sociological Review, 27,* 295-303.

Kiesler, S.B. (1966), 'The effect of perceived role requirements on reactions to favor-doing', *Journal of Experimental Social Psychology, 2,* 198-210.

Kiesler, C.A., Nisbett, R.E. and Zanna, M.P. (1969), 'On inferring one's beliefs from one's behavior', *Journal of Personality and Social Psychology, 11,* 321-7.

Kiesler, S.B. and Baral, R.L. (1970), 'The search for a romantic partner: the effects of self esteem and physical attractiveness on romantic behavior', in K.J. Gergen and D. Marlowe (eds), *Personality and Social Behavior,* Addison-Wesley, Reading, Mass.

Klein, D.C., Fencil-Morse, E. and Seligman, M.E.P. (1976), 'Learned helplessness, depression and the attribution of failure', *Journal of Personality and Social Psychology, 33,* 508-16.

Kline, P. (1972), *Fact and Fantasy in Freudian Theory,* Methuen, London.

Kline, P. (1977), 'The Psychoanalytic Theory of Humour and Laughter', in A.J. Chapman and H.C. Foot (eds), *It's a Funny Thing, Humour,* Pergamon, Oxford.

Koestler, A. (1964), *The Act of Creation,* Dell, New York.

Kubie, L.S. (1971), 'The destructive potential of humour in psychotherapy', *American Journal of Psychiatry, 127,* 861-86.

Kuethe, J.L. (1962), 'Social schemas', *Journal of Abnormal and Social Psychology, 64,* 31-8.
La Fave, L. (1972), 'Humor judgments as a function of reference group and identification classes', in J.H. Goldstein and P.E. McGhee (eds), *The Psychology of Humor,* Academic Press, New York.
La Fave, L. (1977), 'Ethnic humour: From paradoxes towards principles', in A.J. Chapman and H.C. Foot (eds), *It's a Funny Thing, Humour,* Pergamon, Oxford.
La Fave, L., McCarthy, K. and Haddad, J. (1973), 'Humour judgments as a function of identification classes: Canadian versus American', *Journal of Psychology, 85,* 53-9.
La Fave, L., Haddad, J. and Maesen, W.A. (1976), 'Superiority, enhanced self esteem, and perceived incongruity humour theory', in A.J. Chapman and H.C. Foot (eds), *Humour and Laughter: Theory, Research and Applications,* Wiley, London.
Laing, R.D. (1959), *The Divided Self,* Tavistock, London.
Lamm, H. (1967), 'Will an observer advise high risk taking after hearing a discussion of the decision problem?', *Journal of Personality and Social Psychology, 6,* 467-71.
La Piere, R.T. (1934), 'Attitudes vs. actions', *Social Forces, 13,* 230-7.
Lemaine, G. (1974), 'Social differentiation and social originality', *European Journal of Social Psychology, 4,* 17-52.
Lepper, M.R., Greene, D. and Nisbett, R.E. (1973), 'Undermining children's intrinsic interest with extrinsic reward: a test of the "overjustification" hypothesis', *Journal of Personality and Social Psychology, 28,* 129-37.
Levine, J. (1977), 'Humour as a form of therapy', in A.J. Chapman and H.C. Foot (eds), *It's a Funny Thing, Humour,* Pergamon, Oxford.
Levinger, G. and Schneider, D.J. (1969), 'Test of the "risk as a value" hypothesis', *Journal of Personality and Social Psychology, 11,* 165-9.
Lewin, K. (1948), *Resolving social conflicts: selected papers on group dynamics,* Harper, New York.
Losco, J. and Epstein, S. (1975), 'Humor preference as a subtle measure of attitudes towards the same and the opposite sex', *Journal of Personality, 43,* 321-34.
Lott, A.J. and Lott, B.E. (1961), 'Group cohesiveness, communication level and conformity', *Journal of Abnormal and Social Psychology, 62,* 408-12.
McArthur, L.A. (1972), 'The how and what of why: some determinants and consequences of causal attribution', *Journal of Personality and Social Psychology, 22,* 171-93.
McClelland, D., Atkinson, J.W., Clark, R.A. and Lowell, E.L. (1953), *The Achievement Motive,* Appleton Century Crofts, New York.
McDougall, W. (1903), 'The theory of laughter', *Nature, 67,* 318-19.
McGhee, P.E. (1972), 'On the cognitive origins of incongruity humour:

Fantasy assimilation versus reality assimilation', in J.H. Goldstein and P.E. McGhee (eds), *The Psychology of Humour: Theoretical Perspectives and Empirical Issues,* Academic Press, New York.

McGhee, P.E. (1974), 'Cognitive mastery and children's humour', *Psychological Bulletin, 81,* 721-30.

McGhee, P.E. (1977), 'A model of the origins and early development of incongruity-based humour', in A.J. Chapman and H.C. Foot (eds), *It's a Funny Thing, Humour,* Pergamon, Oxford.

McGhee, P.E. (1979), *Humor: its Origin and Development,* Freeman, San Francisco.

McGhee, P.E. (1980), 'Development of the sense of humour in childhood: a longitudinal study', in P.E. McGhee and A.J. Chapman (eds), *Children's Humour,* Wiley, Chichester.

McGhee, P.E. and Chapman, A.J. (1980), 'Children's Humour: Overview and Conclusions', in P.E. McGhee and A.J. Chapman (eds), *Children's Humour,* Wiley, Chichester.

McGuire, M.V. and Bermant, G. (1977), 'Individual and group decisions in response to a mock trial', *Journal of Applied Social Psychology, 7,* 220-6.

McGuire, W.J. (1965), Discussion of William N. Schoenfeld's paper in O. Klineberg and R. Christie (eds), *Perspectives in Social Psychology,* Holt, Rinehart & Winston, New York.

McLachlan, A.J. (1979), 'Categorization of Arguments and Group Polarization', unpublished PhD thesis, University of London.

Marquis, D.C. and Reitz, H.J. (1969), 'Effect of uncertainty in risk taking in individual decisions', *Behavioral Science, 14,* 281-8.

Martineau, W.H. (1972), 'A model of the social functions of humour', in J.H. Goldstein and P.E. McGhee (eds), *The Psychology of Humour,* Academic Press, New York.

Meichenbaum, D.H., Bowers, K.S. and Ross, R.R. (1969), 'A behavioral analysis of teacher expectancy effect', *Journal of Personality and Social Psychology, 13,* 306-16.

Meltzer, B.N., Petras, J.W. and Reynolds, L.T. (1975), *Symbolic Interactionism: Genesis, varieties and criticism,* Routledge & Kegan Paul, London.

Meyers, W.J., Valenstein, E.S. and Lacy, J.I. (1963), 'Heart rate changes after reinforcing brain stimulation in rats', *Science, 140,* 1233-5.

Miller, H. and Geller, D. (1972), 'Structural balance in dyads', *Journal of Personality and Social Psychology, 21,* 135-8.

Mindess, H. (1976), 'The use and abuse of humour in psychotherapy', in A.J. Chapman and H.C. Foot (eds), *Humour and Laughter: Theory, Research and Applications,* Wiley, London.

Mischel, W. (1968), *Personality and Assessment,* Wiley, New York.

Mischel, W. (1973), 'Towards a cognitive social learning reconceptualization of personality', *Psychological Review, 80,* 252-83.

Moscovici, S. (1972), 'Society and Theory in Social Psychology', in

J. Israel and H. Tajfel (eds), *The Context of Social Psychology: A Critical Assessment,* Academic Press, New York.

Moscovici, S. (1976), *Social Influence and Social Change,* Academic Press, London.

Moscovici, S. and Zavalloni, M. (1969), 'The group as a polarizer of attitudes', *Journal of Personality and Social Psychology, 12,* 125-35.

Moscovici, S. and Lage, E. (1976), 'Studies in social influence III: Majority versus minority influence in a group', *European Journal of Social Psychology, 6,* 149-74.

Mower White, C.J. (1977a), 'A limitation of Balance Theory: the effects of identification with a member of the triad', *European Journal of Social Psychology, 7,* 111-16.

Mower White, C.J. (1977b), 'Cognitive complexity and completion of social structures', *Social Behaviour and Personality, 5,* 305-10.

Mower White, C.J. (1979), 'Factors affecting balance, agreement and positivity biases in POQ and POX triads', *European Journal of Social Psychology, 9,* 129-48.

Muchlman, J.T., Bruker, C. and Ingram, C.M. (1976), 'The generosity shift', *Journal of Personality and Social Psychology, 34,* 344-51.

Mugny, G. (1975), 'Negotiations, image of the other and the process of minority influence', *European Journal of Social Psychology, 5,* 209-28.

Murray, H.A. (1938), *Explorations in Personality,* Oxford University Press.

Murstein, B.I. (1961), 'The complementary need hypothesis in newly-weds and middle-aged married couples', *Journal of Abnormal and Social Psychology, 63,* 194-7.

Murstein, B.I. (1971), 'A theory of marital choice and its applicability to marriage adjustment', in B.I. Murstein (ed.), *Theories of Attraction and Love,* Springer, New York.

Mutuma, H., La Fave, L., Mannell, R. and Guilmette, A.M. (1977), 'Ethnic Humour *is* no joke', in A.J. Chapman and H.C. Foot (eds), *It's a Funny Thing, Humour,* Pergamon, Oxford.

Myers, D.G. (1974), 'Social comparison processes in choice dilemma responding', *Journal of Psychology, 86,* 287-92.

Myers, D.G. and Bishop, G.D. (1970), 'Discussion effects on racial attitudes', *Science, 169,* 778-9.

Myers, D.G., Wong, D.W. and Murdoch, P.H. (1971), 'Discussion arguments, information about others' responses and risky shift', *Psychonomic Science, 24,* 81-3.

Myers, D.G., Bach, P.J. and Schreiber, F.D. (1974), 'Normative and informational effects of group interaction', *Sociometry, 37,* 275-86.

Myers, D.G. and Lamm, H. (1976), 'The Group Polarization Phenomenon', *Psychological Bulletin, 83,* 602-27.

Nelson, D. (1965), 'The effect of differential magnitude of reinforcement on interpersonal attraction', unpublished doctoral dissertation, University of Texas.

Nemeth, C. (1976), 'Rules governing jury deliberations: a consideration of recent changes', in G. Bermant, C. Nemeth, and N. Vidmar (eds), *Psychology and the Law,* Lexington Books, Lexington.

Nerhardt, G. (1970), 'Humour and inclination to laugh: Emotional reactions to stimuli of different divergence from a range of expectancy', *Scandinavian Journal of Psychology, 11,* 185-95.

Nerhardt, G. (1976), 'Incongruity and funniness: towards a new descriptive model', in A.J. Chapman and H.C. Foot (eds), *Humour and Laughter: Theory, Research and Applications,* Wiley, London.

Nerhardt, G. (1977), 'Operationalization of incongruity in humour research: a critique and suggestions', in A.J. Chapman and H.C. Foot (eds) *It's a Funny Thing, Humour,* Pergamon, Oxford.

Newcomb, T.M. (1943), *Personality and social change: attitude formation in a student community,* Dryden Press, New York.

Newcomb, T.M. (1953), 'An approach to the study of communicative acts', *Psychological Review, 60,* 393-404.

Newcomb, T.M. (1956), 'The Prediction of interpersonal attraction', *American Psychologist, 11,* 575-86.

Newcomb, T.M. (1959), 'Individual systems of orientation', in S. Koch (ed.), *Psychology: A Study of a Science,* vol. 3, McGraw-Hill, New York, pp. 384-422.

Newcomb, T.M. (1961), *The Acquaintance Process,* Holt, Rinehart & Winston, New York.

Newcomb, T.M. (1968), 'Interpersonal balance', in R.P. Abelson, E. Aronson, W.J. McGuire, T.M. Newcomb, M.J. Rosenberg and P.H. Tannenbaum (eds), *Theories of Cognitive Consistency: A Source Book,* Rand McNally, Chicago.

Nisbett, R.E. and Schachter, S. (1966), 'Cognitive manipulation of pain', *Journal of Experimental Social Psychology, 2,* 227-36.

Nisbett, R.E. and Valins, S. (1971), 'Perceiving the causes of one's own behavior', in E.E. Jones, D.E. Kanouse, H.H. Kelley, R.E. Nisbett, S. Valins and B. Weiner (eds), *Attribution: Perceiving the Causes of Behavior,* General Learning Press, Morristown,

Nisbett, R.E., Caputo, C., Legant, P. and Maracek, J. (1973), 'Behavior as seen by the actor and as seen by the observer', *Journal of Personality and Social Psychology, 27,* 157-64.

Nisbett, R.E. and Wilson, T.D. (1977), 'Telling more than we can know: verbal reports on mental processes', *Psychological Review, 84,* 231-59.

Nuttin, J.M. (1975), *The Illusion of Attitude Change: Towards a Response Contagion Theory of Persuasion,* Academic Press, London.

O'Connell, W.E. (1976), 'Freudian Humour: the eupsychia of everyday life', in A.J. Chapman and H.C. Foot (eds), *Humour and Laughter: Theory, Research and Applications,* Wiley, London.

O'Connell, W.E. (1977), 'The sense of humour: Actualizer of persons and theories', in A.J. Chapman and H.C. Foot (eds), *It's a Funny Thing, Humour,* Pergamon, Oxford.

Orne, M.T. (1962), 'On the social psychology of the psychological experiment with particular reference to the demand characteristics and their implications', *American Psychologist, 17,* 776-83.

Osgood, C.E. and Tannenbaum, P.H. (1955), 'The principle of congruity in the prediction of attitude change', *Psychological Review, 62,* 42-55.

Osmon, B.E. and Mower White, C.J. (1977), 'The importance of both judgmental scales and aspects of an attitudinal issue for dimensional salience', *British Journal of Social and Clinical Psychology, 16,* 123-9.

Paicheler, G. (1976), 'Norms and attitude change I: Polarization and styles of behaviour', *European Journal of Social Psychology, 6,* 405-27.

Parducci, A. (1963), 'Range-frequency compromise in judgment', *Psychological Monographs, 77* (2, whole no. 565).

Peabody, D. (1970), 'Evaluative and descriptive aspects in personality perception: a reappraisal', *Journal of Personality and Social Psychology, 16,* 639-46.

Phares, E.J. (1976), *Locus of Control in Personality,* General Learning Press, Morristown.

Phares, E.J., Wilson, K.G. and Klyver, N.W. (1971), 'Internal-external control and the attribution of blame under neutral and distractive conditions', *Journal of Personality and Social Psychology, 18,* 285-8.

Piaget, J. (1952), *The Origins of Intelligence in Children*, International Universities Press, New York.

Piaget, J. (1962), *Play, Dreams and Imitation in Childhood,* Norton, New York.

Picek, J.S., Sherman, S.J. and Shiffrin, R.M. (1975), 'Cognitive organization and coding of social structures', *Journal of Personality and Social Psychology, 31,* 758-68.

Pien, D. and Rothbart, M.K. (1980), 'Incongruity, Humour, Play and Self-Regulation of Arousal in Young Children', in P.E. McGhee and A.J. Chapman (eds), *Children's Humour,* Wiley, Chichester.

Pollis, N.P. (1967), 'Relative stability of scales formed in individual togetherness and group situations', *British Journal of Social and Clinical Psychology, 6,* 249-55.

Pollis, N.P. and Montgomery, R.L. (1968), 'Individual judgmental stability and the natural group', *Journal of Social Psychology, 74,* 75-81.

Popper, K. (1959), *The Logic of Scientific Discovery*, Basic Books, New York.

Price, K.O., Harburg, E. and Newcomb, T.M. (1966), 'Psychological balance in situations of negative interpersonal attitudes', *Journal of*

Personality and Social Psychology, 3, 265-70.

Pruitt, D.G. (1971), 'Conclusions: toward an understanding of choice shifts in group discussion', *Journal of Personality and Social Psychology, 20,* 495-510.

Rabbie, J.M. and Horwitz, M. (1969), 'Arousal of ingroup bias by chance win or loss', *Journal of Personality and Social Psychology, 13,* 269-77.

Rabbie, J.M. and Visser, L. (1972), 'Bargaining strength and group polarization in intergroup negotiations', *European Journal of Social Psychology, 2,* 401-16.

Radcliffe-Brown, A.R. (1940), 'On joking relationships', *Africa, 13,* 195-210.

Rettig, S. and Turoff, S.F. (1967), 'Exposure to group discussion and predicted ethical risk taking', *Journal of Personality and Social Psychology, 7,* 177-80.

Ring, K. (1967), 'Experimental social psychology: some sober questions about some frivolous values', *Journal of Experimental Social Psychology, 3,* 113-23.

Rodrigues, A. (1965), 'On the differential effects of some of the parameters of balance', *Journal of Psychology, 61,* 240-50.

Rodrigues, A. (1967), 'The effects of balance, positivity and agreement in triadic social relations', *Journal of Personality and Social Psychology, 5,* 472-6.

Rodrigues, A. (1968), 'The biasing effect of agreement in balanced and imbalanced triads', *Journal of Personality, 36,* 138-53.

Rogers, C. (1950), 'The significance of the self-regarding attitudes and perceptions', in M.L. Reymert (ed.), *Feeling and Emotion; The Mooseheart Symposium,* McGraw-hill, New York.

Rogers, C. (1951), *Client-centred Therapy,* Houghton Mifflin, Boston.

Rogers, C. (1959), 'A theory of therapy, personality and interpersonal relationships, as developed in the client-centred framework', in S. Koch (ed.), *Psychology: A Study of a Science,* vol. 3, McGraw-Hill, New York, pp. 184-256.

Rosenberg, M. (1964), 'Parental interest and children's self-conceptions', *Sociometry, 26,* 35-49.

Rosenberg, M. (1965), *Society and the Adolescent Self-Image,* Princeton University Press.

Rosenberg, M. and Simmons, R. (1971), *Black and White Self-Esteem: The Urban School-Child,* American Sociological Association, Washington DC.

Rosenberg, R. (1969), 'The conditions and consequences of evaluation apprehension', in R. Rosenthal and R.L. Rosnow (eds), *Artifact in Behavioural Research,* Academic Press, New York.

Rosenthal, R. and Jacobson, L.F. (1968), 'Teacher expectations for the disadvantaged', *Scientific American, 218,* 19-23.

Rosenthal, R. and Rosnow, R.L. (1969) (eds), *Artifact in Behavioural*

Research, Academic Press, New York.

Ross, M., Insko, C.A. and Ross, H.S. (1971), 'Self-attribution of attitude', *Journal of Personality and Social Psychology, 17,* 292-7.

Rothbart, M.K. (1973), 'Laughter in young children', *Psychological Bulletin, 80,* 247-56.

Rothbart, M.K. (1976), 'Incongruity, problem-solving and laughter', in A.J. Chapman and H.C. Foot (eds), *Humour and Laughter: Theory, Research and Applications,* Wiley, London.

Rothbart, M.K. (1977), 'Psychological approaches to the study of humour' in A.J. Chapman and H.C. Foot (eds), *It's a Funny Thing, Humour*, Pergamon, Oxford.

Rothbart, M.K. and Pien, D. (1977), 'Elephants and Marshmallows: a theoretical synthesis of incongruity-resolution and arousal theories of humour', in A.J. Chapman and H.C. Foot (eds), *It's a Funny Thing, Humour,* Pergamon, Oxford.

Rotter, J.B. (1954), *Social Learning and Clinical Psychology,* Prentice-Hall, Englewood Cliffs, N.J.

Rotter, J.B. (1966), 'Generalized expectancies for internal versus external control of reinforcement', *Psychological Monographs, 80* (1, whole No. 609).

Rubin, Z. (1970), 'The measurement of romantic love', *Journal of Personality and Social Psychology, 16,* 265-73.

Rubin, Z. (1973), *Liking and Loving: An Invitation to Social Psychology,* Holt, Rinehart & Winston, New York.

Rubin, Z. and Zajonc, R.B. (1969), 'Structural bias and generalization in the learning of social structures', *Journal of Personality, 37,* 310-24.

Rubovits, P.C. and Maehr, M.L. (1971), 'Pygmalion analysed: toward an explanation of the Rosenthal-Jacobson findings', *Journal of Personality and Social Psychology, 19,* 197-203.

Rubovits, P.C. and Maehr, M.L. (1973), 'Pygmalion black and white', *Journal of Personality and Social Psychology, 25,* 210-11.

Sampson, E.E. and Insko, C.A. (1964), 'Cognitive consistency and performance in the autokinetic situation', *Journal of Abnormal and Social Psychology, 68,* 184-92.

Sanders, G.S. and Baron, R.S. (1977), 'Is social comparison irrelevant for producing choice shifts?', *Journal of Experimental Social Psychology, 13,* 303-14.

Schachter, S. and Singer, J.E. (1962), 'Cognitive, social and physiological determinants of emotional state', *Psychological Review, 69,* 379-99.

Schroeder, H.E. (1973), 'The risky shift as a general choice shift', *Journal of Personality and Social Psychology, 27,* 297-300.

Schultz, D.P. (1965), *Sensory Restriction: Effects on Behaviour,* Academic Press, New York.

Schutz, A. and Luckmann, T. (1974), *The Structures of the Life World,*

Heinemann, London.

Secord, P.F. (1959), 'Stereotyping and favourableness in the perception of Negro faces', *Journal of Abnormal and Social Psychology, 59,* 309-15.

Secord, P.F. and Backman, C.W. (1965), 'An interpersonal approach to personality', in B. Maher (ed.), *Progress in Experimental Research,* vol. 2, Academic Press, New York.

Secord, P.F. and Backman, C.W. (1974), *Social Psychology* (2nd edn) McGraw-Hill, Tokyo.

Secord, P.F., Bevan, W. and Katz, B. (1956), 'The negro stereotype and perceptual accentuation', *Journal of Abnormal and Social Psychology, 53,* 78-83.

Secord, P.F. and Muthard, J.E. (1955), 'Personalities in faces: II. Individual differences in the perception of women's faces', *Journal of Abnormal and Social Psychology, 50,* 238-42.

Seligman, M.E.P. (1972), 'Learned helplessness', *Annual Review of Medicine, 23,* 407-12.

Seligman, M.E.P. (1975), *Helplessness,* Freeman, San Francisco.

Selltiz, C., Edrich, H. and Cook, S.W. (1965), 'Ratings of favorableness about a social group as an indication of attitude toward the group', *Journal of Personality and Social Psychology, 2,* 408-15.

Sherif, C.W., Sherif, M. and Nebergall, R.E. (1965), *Attitude and Attitude Change: The Social Judgment-involvement Approach,* Saunders, Philadelphia.

Sherif, M. (1935), 'A study of some social factors in perception', *Archives of Psychology, 22,* no.187.

Sherif, M. (1951), 'A preliminary experimental study of intergroup relations', in J.H. Rohrer and M. Sherif (eds), *Social Psychology at the Crossroads,* Harper, New York.

Sherif, M. (1966), *Group Conflict and Co-operation: Their social psychology.* Routledge & Kegan Paul, London.

Sherif, M. and Hovland, C.I. (1961), *Social Judgement: Assimilation and Contrast Effects in Communication and Attitude Change,* Yale University Press, New Haven, Conn.

Sherif, M. and Sherif, C.W. (1953), *Groups in Harmony and Tension,* Harper, New York.

Sherif, M., Taub, D. and Hovland, C.I. (1958), 'Assimilation and contrast effects of anchoring stimuli on judgment', *Journal of Experimental Psychology, 55,* 150-5.

Sherman, S.J. and Wolosin, R.J. (1973), 'Cognitive biases in a recognition task', *Journal of Personality, 41,* 395-412.

Shotter, J. (1978), 'Homo Duplex: the personal and the political', paper presented to the British Psychological Society Social Psychology Conference, September 1978.

Shultz, T.R. (1972), 'The role of incongruity and resolution in children's appreciation of cartoon humour', *Journal of Experimental*

Child Psychology, 13, 456-77.

Shultz, T.R. (1974a), 'Order of cognitive processing in humour appreciation', *Canadian Journal of Psychology, 28,* 409-20.

Shultz, T.R. (1974b), 'Development of the appreciation of riddles', *Child Development, 45,* 100-5.

Shultz, T.R. (1976), 'A cognitive-developmental analysis of humour', in A.J. Chapman and H.C. Foot (eds), *Humour and Laughter: Theory, Research and Applications,* Wiley, London.

Shultz, T.R. and Horibe, F. (1974), 'Development of the appreciation of verbal jokes', *Developmental Psychology, 10,* 13-20.

Shurcliff, A. (1968), 'Judged humour, arousal, and the relief theory', *Journal of Personality and Social Psychology, 8,* 360-3.

Skolnick, P. (1971), 'Reactions to personal evaluation: a failure to replicate', *Journal of Personality and Social Psychology, 18,* 62-7.

Snow, R.E. (1969), 'Unfinished Pygmalion', *Contemporary Psychology, 14,* 197-9.

Soltysik, S. (1960), 'Studies on avoidance conditioning: III Alimentary conditioned reflex model of the avoidance reflex', *Acta Biologiae Experimentalis, 21,* 235-52.

Songer-Nocks, E. (1976), 'Situational factors affecting the weighting of predictor components in the Fishbein model', *Journal of Experimental Social Psychology, 12,* 56-69.

Spencer, H. (1860), 'The physiology of laughter', *Macmillan's Magazine, 1,* 395-402.

Sroufe, L.A. and Waters, E. (1976), 'The ontogenesis of smiling and laughter: a perspective on the organization of development in infancy', *Psychological Review, 83,* 173-89.

Sroufe, L.A. and Wunsch, J.P. (1972), 'The development of laughter in the first year of life', *Child Development, 43,* 1326-44.

Stalling, R.B. (1970), 'Personality similarity and evaluative meaning as conditioners of attraction', *Journal of Personality and Social Psychology, 14,* 77-82.

Stokes, J.P. (1971), 'Effects of familiarization and knowledge of others' odd choice on shifts to risk and caution', *Journal of Personality and Social Psychology, 20,* 407-12.

Stoner, J.A.F. (1961), 'A comparison of individual and group decisions involving risk', unpublished Master's Thesis, M.I.T.

Storms, M.D. (1973), 'Videotape and the attribution process: reversing actors' and observers' points of view', *Journal of Personality and Social Psychology, 27,* 165-75.

Strassberg, D.S. (1973), 'Relationships among locus of control, anxiety and valued-goal expectations', *Journal of Consulting and Clinical Psychology, 41,* 319.

Stroebe, W., Eagly, A.H. and Stroebe, M.S. (1977), 'Friendly or just polite? The effect of self esteem on attributions', *European Journal of Social Psychology, 7,* 265-74.

Sullivan, H.S. (1953), *The Interpersonal Theory of Psychiatry,* Norton, New York.

Suls, J.M. (1972), 'A two-stage model for the appreciation of jokes and cartoons: an information processing analysis', in J.H. Goldstein and P.E. McGhee (eds), *The Psychology of Humour,* Academic Press, New York.

Suls, J.M. (1977), 'Cognitive and disparagement theories of humour: a theoretical and empirical synthesis', in A.J. Chapman and H.C. Foot (eds), *It's a Funny Thing, Humour,* Pergamon, Oxford.

Sutton-Smith, B. (1975), 'A developmental structural account of riddles', in B. Kirschenblatt-Gimblet (ed.), *Speech Play and Display,* Mouton, the Hague.

Swensen, C.H. (1967), 'Psychotherapy as a special case of dyadic interaction: some suggestions for theory and research', *Psychotherapy: Theory, Research and Practice, 4,* 7-13.

Szasz, T.S. (1972), *The Myth of Mental Illness: Foundations of a Theory of Personal Conduct,* Paladin, London.

Tajfel, H. (1959), 'Quantitative judgment in social perception', *British Journal of Psychology, 50,* 16-29.

Tajfel, H. (1969), 'Cognitive aspects of prejudice', *Journal of Social Issues, 25,* 79-97.

Tajfel, H. (1972), 'Experiments in a vacuum', in J. Israel and H. Tajfel (eds), *The Context of Social Psychology: A Critical Assessment,* Academic Press, London.

Tajfel, H. (1978) (ed.), *Differentiation between Social Groups: Studies in the Social Psychology of Intergroup Relations,* Academic Press, London.

Tajfel, H. and Billig, M. (1974), 'Familiarity and categorization in intergroup behaviour', *Journal of Experimental Social Psychology, 10,* 159-70.

Tajfel, H., Flament, C., Billig, M. and Bundy, R.P. (1971), 'Social categorization and intergroup behaviour', *European Journal of Social Psychology, 1,* 149-78.

Tajfel, H., Sheikh, A.A. and Gardner, R.C. (1964), 'Content of stereotypes and the inference of similarity between members of stereotyped groups', *Acta Psychologica, 22,* 191-201.

Tajfel, H. and Wilkes, A.L. (1963), 'Classification and quantitative judgment', *British Journal of Psychology, 54,* 101-14.

Taylor, S.E. (1975), 'On inferring one's attitudes from one's behaviour: some delimiting conditions', *Journal of Personality and Social Psychology, 31,* 126-37.

Teger, A.I. and Pruitt, D.G. (1967), 'Components of group risk taking', *Journal of Experimental Social Psychology, 3,* 189-205.

Thibaut, J.W. and Kelley, H.H. (1959), *The Social Psychology of Groups,* Wiley, New York.

Thomas, W.I. and Znaniecki, F. (1918), *The Polish Peasant in Europe and America,* Badger, Boston.

Thurstone, L.L. (1928), 'Attitudes can be measured', *American Journal of Sociology, 33,* 529-54.

Thurstone, L.L. and Chave, E.J. (1929), *The measurements of attitudes,* University of Chicago Press.

Triandis, H.C. and Fishbein, M. (1963), 'Cognitive interaction in person perception', *Journal of Abnormal and Social Psychology, 67,* 446-53.

Turner, J.C. (1975), 'Social comparison and social identity: some prospects for intergroup behaviour', *European Journal of Social Psychology, 5,* 5-34.

Turner, J.C. (1978), 'Social comparison, similarity and ingroup favouritism', in H. Tajfel (ed.), *Differentiation between Social Groups: Studies in the social psychology of intergroup relations,* Academic Press, London.

Upshaw, H.S. (1962), 'Own attitude as an anchor in equal-appearing intervals', *Journal of Abnormal and Social Psychology, 64,* 85-96.

Upshaw, H.S. (1965), 'The effect of variable perspectives on judgments of opinion statement for Thurstone scales: equal-appearing intervals', *Journal of Personality and Social Psychology, 2,* 60-9.

Upshaw, H.S. (1967), 'Comparison level as a function of reward-cost orientation', *Journal of Personality, 35,* 290-6.

Valins, S. (1966), 'Cognitive effects of false heart-rate feed-back', *Journal of Personality and Social Psychology, 4,* 400-8.

Valins, S. (1972), 'Persistent effects of information about internal reactions: Ineffectiveness of debriefing', in H. London and R.E. Nisbett (eds), *The Cognitive Alteration of Feeling States,* Aldine, Chicago.

Valins, S. and Ray, A.A. (1967), 'Effects of cognitive desensitization on Avoidance Behavior', *Journal of Personality and Social Psychology, 7,* 345-50.

Wallach, M.A. and Kogan, N. (1959), 'Sex differences and judgment processes', *Journal of Personality, 27,* 555-64.

Wallach, M.A., Kogan, N. and Bem, D. (1962), 'Group influence on individual risk taking', *Journal of Abnormal and Social Psychology, 65,* 75-86.

Wallach, M.A., Kogan, N. and Bem, D. (1964), 'Diffusion of responsibility and level of risk taking in groups', *Journal of Abnormal and Social Psychology, 68,* 263-74.

Walster, E., Aronson, V., Abrahams, D. and Rottman, L. (1966), 'Importance of physical attractiveness in dating behaviour', *Journal of Personality and Social Psychology, 4,* 508-16.

Walster, E. and Walster, G.W. (1969), 'The matching hypothesis', *Journal of Personality and Social Psychology, 6,* 248-53.

Watson, D. (1967), 'Relationship between locus of control and anxiety', *Journal of Personality and Social Psychology, 6,* 91-2.

Weiner, B., Frieze, I., Kukla, A., Reed, L., Rest, S. and Rosenbaum, R.M. (1971), 'Perceiving the causes of success and failure', in E.E. Jones, D.E. Kanouse, H.H. Kelley, R.E. Nisbett, S. Valins and B. Weiner (eds), *Attribution: Perceiving the Causes of Behavior,* General Learning Press, Morristown.

Weiner, B. and Kukla, A. (1970), 'An attributional analysis of achievement motivation', *Journal of Personality and Social Psychology, 15,* 1-20.

Wells, L.E. and Marwell, G. (1976), *Self Esteem: Its Conceptualization and Measurement,* Sage, London.

Whitney, R.E. (1971), 'Agreement and positivity in pleasantness ratings of balanced and unbalanced social situations: a cross-cultural study', *Journal of Personality and Social Psychology, 17,* 11-14.

Whyte, W.W. Jr (1956), *The Organization Man,* Simon & Schuster, New York.

Wicker, A.W. (1969), 'Attitudes versus actions: the relationship of overt and behavioral responses to attitude objects', *Journal of Social Issues, 25,* 41-78.

Willems, E.P. and Clark, R.D. (1969), 'Dependence of the risky shift on instructions: a replication', *Psychological Reports, 25,* 811-14.

Wilson, W. and Nakajo, H. (1965), 'Preference for photographs as a function of frequency of presentation', *Psychonomic Science, 3,* 577-8.

Winch, R.F. (1958), *Mate-selection: a Study of Complementary Needs,* Harper & Row, New York.

Wishner, J. (1960), 'Re-analysis of "impressions of personality"', *Psychological Review, 67,* 96-112.

Witkin, H.A., Dyk, R.B., Faterson, H.F., Goodenough, D.R. and Karp, S.A. (1962), *Psychological Differentiation,* Wiley, New York.

Yang, K.S. and Yang, P.H.L. (1973), 'The effects of anxiety and threat on the learning of balanced and unbalanced social structures', *Journal of Personality and Social Psychology, 26,* 201-7.

Yochelson, S. and Samenow, S.E. (1976), *The Criminal Personality,* vols I and 2, Jason Aronson, New York.

Yoshi, N. and Tsukiyama, K. (1952), 'EEG studies on conditioned behaviour of the white rat', *Japanese Journal of Physiology, 2,* 186-93.

Zajonc, R.B. (1968), 'Attitudinal effects of mere exposure', *Journal of Personality and Social Psychology, 9,* 1-27.

Zajonc, R.B. and Burnstein, E. (1965), 'The learning of balanced and unbalanced social structures', *Journal of Personality, 33,* 153-63.

Zajonc, R.B. and Rajecki, D.W. (1969), 'Exposure and affect: a field experiment', *Psychonomic Science, 17,* 216-17.

Zajonc, R.B. and Sherman, S.J. (1967), 'Structural balance and the induction of relations', *Journal of Personality, 35,* 635-50.

Zanna, M.P. and Cooper, J. (1976), 'Dissonance and the Attribution Process', in J.H. Harvey, W.J. Ickes and R.F. Kidd (eds), *New Directions in Attribution Research,* vol. 1, Lawrence Erlbaum Associates, Hillsdale, NJ.

Zavalloni, M. and Cook, S.W. (1965), 'Influence of judges' attitudes on ratings of favorableness of statements about a social group', *Journal of Personality and Social Psychology, 1,* 43-54.

Zigler, E., Levine, J. and Gould, L. (1967), 'Cognitive challenge as a factor in children's humour appreciation', *Journal of Personality and Social Psychology, 6,* 332-6.

Ziller, R.C. (1973), *The Social Self,* Pergamon, Oxford.

Ziller, R.C. and Grossman, S.H. (1967), 'A developmental study of the self-social constructs of normals and the neurotic personality', *Journal of Clinical Psychology, 23,* 15-21.

Ziller, R.C, Hagey, J., Smith, M.D. and Long, B.H. (1969), 'Self-esteem: a self-social construct', *Journal of Consulting and Clinical Psychology, 33,* 84-95.

Ziller, R.C., Megas, J. and DeCencio, D. (1964), 'Self-social constructs of normals and acute neuropsychiatric patients', *Journal of Consulting Psychology, 20,* 50-63.

Zillmann, D. and Cantor, J.R. (1972), 'Directionality of transitory dominance as a communication variable affecting humour appreciation', *Journal of Personality and Social Psychology, 24,* 191-8.

Zillmann, D. and Cantor, J.R. (1976), ' A disposition theory of humour and mirth', in A.J. Chapman and H.C. Foot (eds), *Humour and Laughter: Theory, Research and Applications,* Wiley, London.

Zimmerman, D.H. and Pollner, M. (1971), 'The everyday world as a phenomenon', in J.D. Douglas (ed.), *Understanding Everyday Life,* Routledge & Kegan Paul, London.

Zuckerman, M. (1969), 'Theoretical Formulations, 1', in J.P. Zubek (ed.), *Sensory Deprivation: Fifteen Years of Research,* Appleton Century Crofts, New York.

Index